Computer Networking Beginners Guide

What is the computer network and how to learn it in a simple way? The Easy step by step Guide for beginners

Table of Contents

Introduction

Congratulations on purchasing this book, Computer *Networking Beginners Guide: What is the computer network and how to learn it in a simple way?*
The Easy step by step Guide for beginners, and thank you for doing so.

The internet has turn into a crucial part of our life in the 21st century. The technology has been integrated with our means of living. For most of us, we start our day by checking e-mails and reading or streaming the news on websites, pay bills through our smartphone's apps and we can navigate our bank accounts better now more than ever with online banking. E-commerce has come a long way. As consumers, we now have the ability to purchase almost anything within our fingertips. We also have the ability to research products, read and provide reviews, and look for the best possible deal. For businesses, this means that they now have the ability for a farther reach. Through e-commerce, small businesses now have a better chance of competing with bigger companies, in getting their products to their target market.

Most schools have incorporated the internet to everyone's advantage. Aside from online portals where students can access school-related materials, teachers can now also communicate with the parents or guardians through email, bridging more connections instead of missed phone calls. A good number of universities, colleges, and trade schools are now offering Distance Education; which is focused on non-traditional students (mostly students who, for any reason, cannot physically attend a class at all times), classes are done via web-stream and student web portals. The end result ranges from a class credit to a certificate, diploma, a bachelor's degree, even a post graduate degree.

Perhaps the most influential contribution the internet has provided is social media. Through it, it somehow made our world a bit smaller, most of us closer. Facebook has reconnected us with our childhood friends, dear relatives we haven't seen in a while, and it has given most of us a way to be connected to our line of interests through groups. Twitter started with only 160 characters per post, since we have the choice on who to follow, we can curate our timeline and be informed of what interests us. The symbol # is WAS more commonly known as the number sign, or pound sign. Today's generation can recognize the sign better as "hashtag". A symbol that has the ability to catapult a topic or a person to the limelight or at least to people's online radar. Social media has become an industry on its own.

Gone are the days when the internet was thought was viewed to be a luxury or a "craze that will fade away". The technology has become so integrated with our lives that the United Nations made a declaration on 2011 that internet access as an important component of a basic human right.

Computer networking is an essential framework for the internet to work for most of us. The tech term can be overwhelming for some, but it exists in almost every home, offices, businesses and establishment that is connected to the internet.

In this book, we will discuss the most basic principles behind computer networking without the complexities of technical jargon (technical terms will be explained). Visual representations will be provided to expound on the technical concepts.

This book is written for anyone who wants an introductory course on computer networking, which is basically what is needed if you want to create a simple home network or office computer network.

Chapter 1: What is Computer Networking

What is networking?

The term "networking" is, by all means, to exchange information or the action or process of interacting with others.

What is Computer Networking?

Computer Networking may sound intimidating or can be overwhelming at first, but the advancements in technology have gone a long way. The graphical user interface (GUI) has become simpler for most operating systems (OS) making it easier to understand and navigate through.

Network is a set of computers connected together with common objective of sharing resources and those resources can be the internet, a printer, or a file server.

Computing is the process of utilizing computer technology to complete a task and the task can be as simple as swiping a credit card or making a call or sending an email. Computing involves the use of computer systems like a laptop, a smartphone, a desktop computer, or even an ATM, basically almost any other smart electronic device.

Computer network involves the use of computers for computing and telecommunication technology like telephone lines, wireless radio links for transmitting the processed data over long distances so the computer network is said to be evolved at the interface of telecommunications and computing.

The first computer that appeared was a TA (terminal adapter) network in a joint geographically distributed computers to each other that word area network is now more commonly known as the internet.

Network is a collection of computers linked together with the goal of allocating resources and those resources can be the internet, a printer, or a file server.

Computing is the process of utilizing computer technology to complete a task and the task can be as simple as swiping a credit card or making a call or sending an email. Computing involves the use of computer systems like a laptop, a smartphone, a desktop computer, or even an ATM, basically almost any other smart electronic device.

Computer network involves the use of computers for computing and telecommunication technology like telephone lines, wireless radio links for transmitting the processed data over long distances so the computer network is said to be evolved at the interface of telecommunications and computing.

The first computer that appeared was a TA network in a joint geographically distributed computers to each other that word area network is now more commonly known as the internet.

Wi-Fi

The word Wi-Fi is derived from the term "wireless fidelity". This type of connection is particularly useful for laptops, smartphones, and other mobile devices that may come and go. Wi-Fi networks rely on a wireless access point through which all traffic must flow the Wireless Access Point creates an area around it known as a hotspot. The Wireless Access Point is effectively a substitute for the backbone cable. If the wireless access point is connected to another network. For example, a much larger wired network or even the internet then it is known as a router.

Local Area Network (LAN)

The computers and other devices are geographically close together with this . This means that computers are usually are in the same town or the same city. In fact, computers in this kind of setup are usually on the same site. For example, all of the computers in an office or all of the computers on campus. Desktop computers in a LAN are usually connected via cable but if there are laptop users as well, then it can possibly connect using W-Fi. One of the biggest advantages of using LAN is it can be used only by the people who are allowed to use it. It is private and secure.

Wide Area Network

This type of network works on a much bigger scale than a LAN. The computers are geographically remote. The network might span an entire city, a country. The devices on the web are usually connected using leased telecommunication lines or satellite links. Signals on WAN will probably be encrypted but it is still less secure than a LAN.

Servers

These are the most powerful computers on a network. They allow the users to share files, applications and peripheral devices. Servers authenticate users to the network when they log on, they have to type in a username and password. Servers can provide email services, can also host private websites known as intranets.

What is not a Computer Network?

Stand-alone computer, which is not connected to any other computers
May have peripheral devices connected like a printer but it cannot communicate with any other computers.

Computers on a network are often referred to as workstations. For a setup like a peer-to-peer network the ensemble of computers have equal status or no server or if all the workstations share files and peripheral devices, they can all be thought of as servers.

Connections between devices on a network can be made using radio signals, this is known as Wi-Fi network.

Advantages of stand-alone computers

- No reliance on servers for files and peripherals
- Faster access to local files
- No need to logon
- More secure than network computers
- Cheaper than network computers

Advantages of networked computers

- Can share files, peripheral devices and even applications
- Communication services such as email and web pages
- Easy to install software onto workstations from a central location
- Easy to set up new users and peripheral devices
- Roaming users can access their own files and settings from anywhere
- Users can have different levels of access to shared resources

Disadvantages of networked computers

- Can be expensive to set up and manage
- Requires specialist skills to keep running
- If the network stops, it may not be possible to access shared resources
- Difficult to secure from hackers or even industrial espionage
- Performance degrades as traffic increases, unless well designed

Chapter 2: History of the Internet

It can be mind-boggling, and anyone can get curious easily as to how we have arrived at a present time where almost countless number of computing devices are all linked together via this extraordinary framework that we all know as the internet. Starting at the initial efforts at organizing computers to function together up to the contemporary inventions like social media networks and video conferences that can be accessed easily, the history and journey of the internet has come a long way.

The design and process making stage took decades to achieve a balanced nature of both software and hardware technology, so this part of the discussion is not going to focus on each single influential inventor and apparatus but we will focus and shed more light on a number of essential design proposals and pivotal moments that have taken the internet technology to this day.

It has been 75 years since World War II and the public has been trying to facilitate to have computers to work together since these days.
This is during a period when computing devices are described to be as huge and awkward - looking equipment that was only

capable of solving complex mathematical problems, nothing more than that.

Richard Feynman, a physicist, led a team that was able to formulate an avenue to solve a big batch of mathematical problems simultaneously. Efficiency was also being advocated during this period, whenever a computing device is not at work, they had it use and delegate it to work on a separate section of a different problem. One mathematical problem might take months to get solved but at the same time, they could also finish multiple math equations in the same period. Whenever they are faced with a critical calculation, they utilized the systems concurrently to do the same problem numerous amounts of times.

This was their means of quality control and be certain of the final answer, even a couple of computing devices are capable of having mistaken once in a while.

Colleges have begun segregating their computer terminals during the early 1950s and 60s. This is when some would experiment programs onto the computers directly. By separating their computer terminals, it made it almost effortless for some to play around and do some trials on new computing devices while safeguarding the circuits and tubes off from tampering.

It can be compared or somehow similar structure of our present day's cloud computing, complicated tasks are being sent away to be worked on by computing machines that are located somewhere else. In order for the modern cloud computing to function, it is essential to have an internet connection for it to work unlike in 1960 when it wasn't the case.

ARPA or the advance Research Project Agency was created by the Department of Defense of the US (today the agency is called Defense Advanced Research Project Agency or DARPA), its goal is to retain its advancement of technology more advanced than the Soviets. Joseph Licklider, who is a renowned American psychologist and computer scientist, took an important role by helping to persuade ARPA to allocate budget for computer network research by bringing together engineers and computer scientists across the country. A number of colleges signed on with the project and in 1969 the construction of the framework was initiated by ARPA. The name ARPANET was given to the technological infrastructure. The network was first of its kind during this period. Though it started small-scale, it functions as a means of messaging service across computers at various universities like the University of Utah, UC Santa Barbara, Stanford University and UCLA.

Engineers kept on increasing the features and their ability to solve problems as the ARPANET continues to expand over the next few decades. Some of these innovations have influenced the manner of what we do online to this day. Packet switching is one of the first major modification done by ARPANET.

[Backstory: In the old days, as you can also see in movies set in the olden times, whenever a person wants to get in touch with somebody via the phone, the first step is to dial and reach a switchboard. Phones during this period could only work because of circuit switching - only when there is a single uninterrupted circuit available can a signal get from one point to another; this is the reason why operators were needed for this form of communication to work. An operator is responsible to move and connect cables from one phone's port into the wire from another one. The idea behind circuit switching is good only if two points are connected for an extended period of time, most landlines still work through this method except today there is no need for operators since circuit switching can be done automatically.]

It would be unwise and unattainable for the internet to perform as how circuit switching did decades ago. If this were the case today - it would take an enormous amount of time for a computer to connect to another digital device and to repeat the process all over. Fortunately, websites of today are capable of connecting a user to computers across the group, up to 10 computers at a time. Simultaneously while monitoring and connecting countless of visitors all at once, it is important that all of these computers respond immediately whenever a user clicks on it. So, in this made-up scenario, it just would not work because of the circuits that are scattered all over the place, it would always be jerking around and connecting to a point for a millisecond before getting disconnected and be misplaced and connected somewhere else.

Computer engineers were made aware as early as the 1960s that computers are capable of sending messages in a far speedy way in order for circuit switching to be practical. Engineers found a way to solve this and invented a substitute way: packet switching, where various computing devices can dispatch messages within the constant set of wires rather than obtaining each separately.

A message called the packet is dispatched within the wires is the method of how to communicate with each other. The address label was assigned to each and every packet.

A set of numbers characterizing the computer where it was going to. The computing device where it began would search the address on a table that contains all the addresses within the network and then dispatches the packet to the nearest computer to the destination. That second computer would receive the packet, search the destination address, and again dispatch the packet to the correct path. This process would be repeated until the packet ultimately reaches its destination. In this process, there was no need to move circuits or wires, it was simultaneous.

The packets of ARPANET moved through phone lines and have utilized packet switching since the beginning. The technology performed as to how it was designed. However, as the year progresses, there were challenges that were encountered along the way.

The number of computers across the country that has joined was surprising. Every computer was somehow required to keep up with the updates list of computer addresses, this is the result of how the packet switching was initially designed. If a computer has failed to update its list, it might receive the packets but may not know the correct patch where to dispatch or forwards it to an address that does not exist anymore. As time went by, it was no longer surprising as to how the network structure kept getting vaster by the minute. There were instances when a computer's address might possibly be altered if it temporarily detaches itself from the network or there was a malfunction within a connection. If the updates were not done fast enough, some computers could end up with different and incorrect address books.

Stanford University was selected by the ARPANET's engineering team as a formal record-keeper of addresses back in 1973. ARPANET has resolved to move on from the problematic system and wanted to keep it more organized. The effectivity of ARPANET's solution has resulted in an increase, with only sixty computers before 1975 that number grew to more than a hundred computing devices by late 1977.

ARPANET was able to stretch its reach to Hawaii from California via satellites. This was remarkable since Hawaii was once considered to be an isolated place at time. ARPANET went further its reach by extending its infrastructure and placed networks in Norway and England.

Comparable networks began to appear across the world, some became more competitive since some had more computing capabilities on them. Around the mid-seventies, the market share was no longer solely owned by ARPANET.

During this period, the packets were formatted differently by each company, as a result even though a user could connect and work with various networks together, it was not functioning as it was originally planned.

The problem at hand was not ironed out until 1974, however, it wasn't until the first part of the eighties when ARPANET and the majority of the networks began utilizing it.

A series of rules named Transmission Control Protocol / Internet Protocol or TCP/IP, which is still being utilized up to this day was the solution that was designed.

The Transmission Control Protocol is a means to standardize how packets were being formatted, in order to have uniformity with how everyone was communicating using the same "language". Internet Protocol is the definitive method of allocating addresses, this is to avoid any error on where the packets should be directed. By the time when both networks began using TCP/IP, communicating and connecting across networks became uncomplicated. The entire existing networks in operations were interconnected, as a result, forming what became recognized as the - INTERNET, with ARPANET as the backbone of it all.

The record-keepers at Stanford began getting overwhelmed with the workload as a result of how fast ARPANET was thriving and needing to connect to various networks at the same time. There was a constant need to update the address book and download its most recent version because of the ever-changing addresses brought by number of hosts that repeatedly joined. In some cases, there were botched communication across the network as a result of the errors in the Stanford list.

In 1971 another form of communication was invented, the email. Two years after it was invented, seventy-five percent of ARPANET's entire packets were comprised of emails. Computers had various email programs during this period, a table of every computer it would pass through across the sender and the receiver; were sometimes required.

During this period, computer users had to have an up to date map of the entirety of the network handy with them. It was necessary for them to key in the path of the email in order for them to send it. The growing number of computers that were on ARPANET, at this point within hundreds and over a thousand that were on the internet, sustaining the most recent maps and its information were becoming a hopeless task.

The engineers of ARPANET have figured out that the total infrastructure of the internet had to be systematically coordinated. The Domain Name System was a part of their solution. The hosts were classified into domains, rather than dichotomizing every host and saving its address in a casual order.

Initially, the domains that were classified as top-level arrived. Email addresses are now ending with either ".com" and ``.edu". Before there was DNS, the way to send an email was just to type in "sam@example" but the new top-level domains meant in order to send an email, the address should be written with an extension like "sam@example.com". Second-level domain was called within each host, for example, "ucla.edu" means the second-level domain is ucla" while the top-level is ".edu". The domain infrastructure has standardized and coordinated all those various hosts across the globe in such a manner that computers could deal with. The DNS's sole responsibility is to keep an account of all addresses and connections; this adds an entirely different network to the internet.

How it works is a computer that lies on the new network adequately saves all the addresses within the dot-com top-level domain. A separate computer has all the dot-edu addresses. Another independent computer houses all the dot-org, and that is how the system works. Other computing devices have the ability to jointly charted out the complete network. As a result, whenever a user wants to send an email, it is no longer required to refer to the map and chart out all the required connections by the user. That has been the purpose of the DNS.

At the onset, they just preferred a couple of dependable interconnected computing devices, but it resulted in performing as the foundation of a universal network of a high number of companies, government, and universities all communication with each other. It was determined to put a closure on the ARPANET project, it was a necessity for them to discover a replacement that will take charge of all the infrastructure, someone to manage the internet.

Big questions came up immediately:
With all this power, can anyone be trusted with it?
Can the general public still have access to the internet which by itself is a massive and perplexing system?

A few companies began to market access to the networks by the 1970s, this is almost the first glimpse into the future of internet use.

The users had the ability to do almost everything; from sending emails, to playing games, chatting on instant messaging programs, and even checking weather reports. However, these were standalone networks and were not attached to the main network that was the internet. It was as good as it gets.

On some that works like Compu Serve, Micronet users had the luxury of reading the news at the comfort of their home via their computers.

During that period those networks were as great as it could for its end-users. However, it still had its limitations, the availability of Micronet was only during the nights and weekends - this is when most businesses that usually utilize the CompuServe's networks are not in operation.

Since they were not precisely interconnected with each other or to the wider internet, it was comparable to being isolated islands.

During the eighties, regardless of the size or expansion of the privatized networks, they were still restricted to be "on the internet".

ARPANET and other founding networks consist of the foundation of the internet was funded and managed by the government, hence any other organizations like universities and private businesses that were permitted to use the network were not authorized to conduct any commercial traffic within the network.

The internet was permitted to be used to download data or send an email of a thesis or a report to your cohorts, but it was not permitted to use for the promotion of a new product and certainly were not permitted to demand payment from the general public to come online. The internet was initially meant for research and development and not for commercialization.

It came to appear that the National Science Foundation's huge network - NSFNET to be the best option to take over the responsibilities from ARPANET and be in charge of the internet. It began in 1986 and expanded rapidly following the connection to ARPANET that within that year, it warranted a considerable number of upgrades to manage all the new traffic.

By the year 1990, NSFNET formally took over ARPANET as the internet's foundation, along with it came its approximately half a million end users. Prior to ARPANET being removed from the scene, a few private companies were connecting members of the general public to the internet.

Initially, NSFNET had a procedure in place regarding forbidding commercial traffic on its network. This policy has changed by 1988 when they have concluded to allow a number of private network's email server to connect to the NSFNET.

In 1989, the first commercial email could be sent across the internet by the users of Compu Serve and MCI Mail - an email service.

In the same year, the first Internet Service Providers (ISP) came to the scene. These were private companies that typically do not own any network, they just facilitate the connection of their customers to the internet and to a local network.

In between the late eighties and early nineties, there were a number of internet service providers that presented various service options from one another; there was an option available that just offers email service, some other options were their privately-owned network that was partially connected to the internet and some presented internet access but with the absence of their own online community. By 1995, ARPANET has ceased its operations for good and transitioned the entire operations to the ISPs.

In the first part of the nineties, for someone to connect to the network, the computer needs a modem in order to place a phone call to the network, the job of the modem is to translate or decode the signals being used by the computer an by the telephone. Computers were utilizing digital signal whilst the landline phone was working on analog signals. The next step is the computer would try to communicate with another set of computers that are on the network by means of the phone lines connecting them. This method of getting online is better known as the dial-up connection. In comparison to how fast our internet works today, the dial-up connection can be described as extremely slow. However, during that time when this was the only method of getting online, it does the job pretty well. Phone lines were active and had a broad coverage across the country when ARPANET came to the scene, it became a logical and cost-efficient decision to utilize the existing phone lines rather than attempting to create something entirely new or invent something else from the ground up. A major factor as to why the dial-up connection was ultra-slow is the existing limitation of how fast a user can compress data down into a phone line. To be able to dispatch and transmit a good amount of data, what is needed is a signal with a categorically high frequency, this means it can quickly change. An extreme high-pitched sound is needed in order for a signal to be sent down through the phone lines. When phone lines were first invented and engineered, it was meant for the phone communications - phone calls. It was not designed to manage the type of signal that the dial-up connection does have. Whenever a modem establishes a connection to a network, its first task is to monitor the signal with the highest frequency that the wires could possibly manage to handle, then it decelerates the channel of ones and zeroes heading from the computer down to that speed.

When the first batch of internet service providers arrived on the scene, the internet could be described as a bit different than it is today. A major reason behind this is the fact that in 1989 the Web was not in existence yet, more so as a single website. Though a lot of people today have been using the terms "internet" and "web" interchangeably, these two words actually are different from one another. It was a decade later until the Web was introduced to the market. The term "internet" is derived from "internetworking", the word came about during the seventies to specify the connecting of the tangible cables and computing devices altogether. The concept behind the internet originated with it being designed as a method of accessing computers, sharing files and programs remotely.

It was getting more challenging to maneuver and move across the network despite knowing where you are supposed to go, this was a direct result of the growing internet community. In 1989, Tim Berners-Lee, a scientist, along with some assistance from his cohort Robert Caillou began on a more efficient avenue to organize all that data. Tim Berners-Lee is frequently attributed as the one who invented the web. Berners-Lee had a big concept to systematize and somehow deflate the multi-branch structure. Rather than having each file being placed separately on its own remote branch, any file could direct the user to other similar or related data files in other for the user to seamlessly navigate one place to the next. There was only one tool that Berners-Lee had in mind that could take this task and it was the - HYPERTEXT.

In the sixties, a protocol called the Hypertext was invented as a means of navigating from one section of a document to a different part, when more users began to utilize it to connect various documents. By the eighties, it was assimilated into majority of programs being used. Berners-Lee incorporated the hypertext in the web developing process and made it the primary method of navigating the web which was later referred to as the "World Wide Web". Because of hyperlinks' ability to connect and ease the navigation through web pages, the web was definitely a sensation at CERN (the European Organization for Nuclear Research). In 1993, web technology was made available to the general public; the last crucial piece of the internet technology of today was put in place.

The concept of utilizing the hypertext protocol is the basis behind most websites having URL that begins with "HTTP" or "HTTPS" (its secured version). HyperText Transfer Protocol is the set of rules, standards, and procedures that are being utilized to inspect and decode files that contains a hyperlink.
The ::// is a method of presenting to the system what is coming up next and "www" is sign that tells the user that the page is a part of the World Wide Web.

New assortments of programs have emerged to open these contemporary hyperlinked web pages. The specifics of each program rely on what the user needs or wants - these were the previous versions of web browsers. The year was 1994 and a browser called - the Netscape was initially launched. The code for this browser was ultimately integrated into another browser which most internet users of today might be familiar with - Firefox. During this time, both the internet and web ultimately partnered up and became easily available and attainable for the public; as a result, the tally of computers utilizing the internet has surged exceedingly.

Due to the sudden increase of computer users in the nineties, during this decade, investments worth billions were cascaded into internet-based startup enterprises.

Investors riled up behind companies like eToys.com, govWorks and WorldCom - a majority of these companies took a hard fall and had to file for bankruptcy by the end of the decade, this is around the same time when ".com bubble" have popped and went out.

The web of the mid to late nineties was a bit like the Wild West, it was a huge new world of people and companies popping up everywhere you looked, and it seemed like there was plenty of room for everyone to have a piece of the pie. A lot of wealthy investors started piling money into companies without worrying about whether they were making a profit or even if they had many customers. The mentality of some during this period was: that being on the internet, old rules for being cautious about investing in young companies did not apply and more, and that all anyone needed was a good idea and enough money to reach an audience.

This period did not last as long as everyone wanted, and what is known as ".com bubble" started bursting in March of 2000. Stocks in tech companies plummeted for the next couple of years, over half of them declared bankruptcy, eventually losing trillions of dollars in total as an industry.

A couple of famous court cases against Microsoft and the music-downloading service Napster put new boundaries on what companies could do with the internet. Napster had been one of the fastest-growing businesses in the tech history, but it went bankrupt paying back musicians for copyright infringement. Microsoft, on the other hand, narrowly avoided being dissolved after violating antitrust laws.

Another one of the ".com bubble" casualties was GeoCities, one of the first social networking sites. Today's web is flooded with social networking, most of us would not be able to imagine going through a day or at the minimum a week without checking at least one social media site. Today, just about every website constantly encourages everyone to use their personal profiles and share everything they see with everyone they know. But things were different back in 1994, when GeoCities first came online. The first websites of the nineties mostly had a clear divide between creators and users. Creators - they wrote the computer code and assembled different documents and files and hyperlinks and pictures that made the website what it was. Users - they just visited the website and looked at whatever the creators had put on there. GeoCities worked on a different model. Anyone and everyone could make a GeoCities account and create their own website, with all their own stuff and formatting and backgrounds and interests. GeoCities mixed together users and creators because everyone with an account was both at the same time. Its users could also send each other messages and joins communities of pages with similar topics and interests, creating a whole section of the site that focused on just about everything imaginable. Its 19 million users made GeoCities the third most popular site on the web in 1999 behind AOL and Yahoo!. The latter bought GeoCities that same year for 3.6 billion dollars, but it fell on hard times during the ".com bubble" crash and has never managed to regain its former glory again. Yahoo! finally shut down most of GeoCities back in 2009 when it had long-since been surpassed by other sites that took the idea of social networking and ran with it. GeoCities gave way to some sites that pretty much everyone can easily recognize today. Friendster launched in 2002 giving each user their own profile and a way of seeing different networks of friends on the site. It quickly became popular, with three million accounts in its first three months. But it was plagued by technical troubles and after a couple of years, it had fewer users than Myspace, which was itself passed in 2008 by Facebook. The number of active users of Facebook has reached almost 2 billion and that number just keeps going up. But it is far from being the only social media site out there today - there's Reddit, Twitter, Tumblr, LinkedIn, YouTube, not even counting all the Disqus comments sections and Digg share buttons and WordPress blogs all over the web - all of these sites, big or small are descended from GeoCities: the first site mix users and creators in a completely new way of using the internet.

Most people still use dial-up to get online in the heydays of GeoCities and Friendster. By the time Myspace took over around 2005, there was something new on the market. Instead of using dial-up, most people had switched over to broadband. Since dial-up has a built-in speed limit, because of how phone lines were made, the fastest dial-up connection could only receive or transmit about 56 kilobits per second. To put that into perspective, that's about 56,000 ones and zeros in or out of the computer every second. With a dial-up speed, downloading a sing song off Napster would take about ten minutes, even at top speed. Downloading a whole movie could take days. Even just loading a site with a few images took a long time. Since the internet was getting more and more popular, companies came up with better ways of getting online that were not so limited.

Like DSL, which transmits digital data along phone lines instead of analog signals like dial-up does; and cable internet, which uses the wires for a cable box to connect to the internet. These newer technologies came to be known as broadband, which is really a broad term for all the ways of getting online that are not dial-up. Depending on the type of broadband, the connections can be tens or hundreds or even thousands of times faster than dial-up is. People started using broadband in the early 2000s, and in 2005 it overtook dial-up as the most popular way Americans got online.

With more people on faster connections, it was no longer a big of a deal for sites to have lots of images or even video being displayed. However, all the data on those sites needed to be stored somewhere. Another legacy of the ".com bubble" is the place of Data Center in today's internet, where hundreds of computers work together for a single company to give users a better and faster experience. The earliest computers could be big enough to take up entire rooms, but those dedicated computer rooms stuck around in a lot of places even as computers for smaller and faster. A sample set up would be like - ten computers, all connected together to act like one big computer with the combined speed and memory of all ten. Lots of the earlier startups needed computer space to store all their data and computer speed to handle all the user traffic in their websites - data centers were perfect for this job. Instead of owning, powering cooling, and maintaining your own computers, and reliably connecting all of them together and to the internet, you could just pay a data center to manage this job. Today's websites have more than a hundred and fifty times as much data on them as they did in 1995, and a lot of that information comes from these data centers that could be in a room or building or whole complexes full of computers. Today's web relies on these huge collections of computers to work like we all expect it to. Because of all the speed and storage available today, websites can now do things they could never have back in 1995.

After the ".com bubble" have gone away, the incident has paved the way for a tamer and steadier web in its wake. Few well-run companies could quietly become empires.

Startups like Google, Amazon, and Facebook began to grow as giant corporations and have started to dominate the market, they have their hands on just about everything you can do online - from search, to advertising, to storage, just to name a few. These websites get about 600 million visitors a year, with hundreds of millions more seeing their ads or using their apps.

Whenever you browse a website like YouTube, even if you're not signed in, you're the only one in the world who sees that exact same YouTube homepage, with those exact recommended videos. This is probably because no one has watched the same video you have, in the same order, for the same amount of time, from the same places in the world - all the stuff that YouTube uses to choose what to recommend. This is similar to when you see banner ads everywhere for products you were just looking at Amazon. Just about everywhere on the web has this sort of algorithmic filtering, where the website decides on what you are probably interested in and shows you more stuff like that. Data centers don't just store all the website's data; they run special programs to look through that data and use information that they have saved about you to decide what you want to see, buy or whatever you might be interested next. Figuring out what you want to see can involve tracking you around the internet. A lot of people have been worried about their privacy - especially because some companies are not shy about selling what they learn about people to the highest bidder. It seems like every day there is another news story about people being tracked around the internet in a similar way.

In a little over fifty years, the internet's grown from four computers to billions. From having connected just within the United States now onto every continent and even into outer space. We can say it is still new and it is still evolving. One thing is for sure, it is exciting what the technology of the future holds for us.

Chapter 3: Components of a Computer Network

Internet Technology

Broadband Cable Internet

Cable internet is a high-speed access technology which utilizes a cable modem with an attached coaxial cable which provides a link to the internet service provider (ISP). Broadband cable is commonly furnished by the same provider that lends cable television to their customer. Because it is provided by cable television providers, broadband cable leverages on the existing infrastructure from cable TV to cover large geographical areas, especially here in the United States. Most cable providers offer different packages vary in speed. Download speed can vary from anywhere from 25 megabits per second all the way up to 400 megabits per second.

If you were to order cable internet for your home or even home office, your cable internet provider would send you modem but more recently they have been sending a modem with a Wi-Fi router combo which is often referred to as a gateway. A device could be a modem with built-in switch and Wi-Fi router, all in one. This modem requires the user to attach a coaxial cable that is routed to the home and then it needs to be attached to the back of the device. The modem is what delivers the internet into a house, the switch and the Wi-Fi router is there so the user can connect multiple wired wireless devices such as computers, laptops, tablets, and smartphones and provide it with the internet access.

Cable broadband does have a downside, because the houses in the same neighborhood will all have to share a pull of bandwidth that is being provided by the cable provider with that specific area. It means that during peak hours, time when a lot of devices are online and using bandwidth, users may experience a slowdown in the internet speed.

DSL Internet

The DSL or Digital Subscriber Line is a popular technology, used by most homes and businesses to access broadband data over the internet. DSL can carry both voice and data at the same time over phone lines. It uses a modem where a common telephone line (rj45) to carry its data. Since this technology uses phone lines, it is far-off in comparison to the older technology - dial up connection. DSL is a high-speed connection that is faster than dial up connection, and in this technology the user can go on the internet and talk on the landline phone at the same time. In case you're not familiar with dial up connection, you can only do phone call OR be on the internet but can never do both at the same time if using the same connection.

DSL is not as fast as cable internet, but it is more affordable from the price point. There is no need to share bandwidth within a neighborhood or block, everyone who is using DSL has their own dedicated connection. It is not a shared line.

In terms of availability, DSL is widely accessible to users because it uses common telephone lines which are nearly everywhere. The internet speed on DSL can vary depending on the area, but on average it can offer download speeds anywhere from 5 megabits per second up to 100 megabits per second. The DSL modem typically comes as a modem and Wi-Fi router combo, it requires the user to plug a standard phone line with a phone jack at the back of the DSL modem.

Asymmetric Digital Subscriber Line (ADSL)

- The download speed is considerably faster than the upload speed
- This is ideal for home-use. Typically, home users download a lot more than upload
- Most affordable form of DSL

Symmetric Digital Subscriber Line (SDSL)

- As the name implies, the download and upload speeds are the same level
- Ideal for business-use

Very High Bit Rate Digital Subscriber Line (VDSL)

- Fast form of DSL that also runs over copper wire
- Since it uses copper wire, it is more effective for short distance
- VDSL is roughly three times faster than ADSL

Fiber Internet

This type of internet technology offers the fastest internet speeds available today. It has download and upload speeds that can reach as fast as 1,000 megabits per second. The reason why this type of connection is extremely fast is because it uses light to send data running through fiber optic cable. Fiber optic cable is what is already being used as the backbone of the internet.

Aside from speed, fiber internet can also travel much longer distances than DSL or cable. The reason behind is; DSL and cable transmit data using electricity over copper cable and signals in copper cable can be affected by electromagnetic interference as it travels which can weaken the signal, especially over a long distance. Fiber internet, on the other hand, uses light to transmit its data through a thin glass cable which makes it less vulnerable to interference.

Physical Components of a Computer Network

Internet is but a network of computing devices allowing us to send messages, make voice calls, video calls, online shopping, and other similar tasks online, but what are the physical components of this computer network which are helping us to perform all these activities?

- **End Points** - includes personal computers, phones, tablets, printers, servers, or any other devices that users need. Servers are data centers used to sort it out that can be shared with other devices. Servers also provides information while other devices retrieve information. End Points can both provide or retrieve information

- **Network Interface Card (NIC)** - To retrieve information of you Facebook account from the Facebook server, you will need to type www.facebook.com in your web browser. This request is first converted to a format which can reach facebook.com; The server device which carries out this conversion process is called network interface card. Port to which to connect a LAN cable in our computers is embedded in a network interface card. All endpoints have a network interface card, either wired or wireless. The NIC of an endpoint can convert data to electrical signals, light signals, or radio signals.

- **Network Media** - It provides means through which data from a NIC of one device is transmitted to and NIC of the other device and it can be a LAN cable for transmitting electrical signals, optical fiber for transmitting light signals, or air in case of radio signals.

- **Connectors** - Connectors provides connection points for a network media.

- **LAN Cables** - are connected to network interface cards of computers using rj45 connectors. All devices in the internet are connected to each other using connectors and network media.

- **Switch** - Network switch is a multi-port device which assures data will go to the right destination within the local area network.

  For a local area network, various equipment and gadgets are linked to each other using another network component called Switch. A SOHO network or small office home office network typically uses single network switch to connect multiple devices.

- **Router** - To access internet networks which is further connected to a device called a router.

  The internet is consisting of a large number of interconnected routers and all of these routers perform two basic functions. First is to connect different networks, second is to provide the best path to access the requested content.

A typical computer network may include endpoints, network interface card, network media, connectors, switches, and routers as physical components.

Pretty much all computer networks these days are using Ethernet, it is a system by which devices can exchange data on a network. Data is broken up and packaged into small pieces by the sending computer. These packages are known as frames. Frames are then transmitted individually. It is convenient to think of a stream of frames on the cable rather like sticks floating on a river. In reality, each frame is a burst of high and low voltages which represents the ones and zeros of binary encoded data. The sending computer's network interface card (NIC) is responsible for generating the rapid pulses of electricity that make up each frame. Whenever a frame is transmitted by a computer, it is actually broadcasting the frame on the network, every other computer can see the frame but only the intended recipient, the one with the correct destination MAC address chooses not to ignore it. At any instant, a cable either has a voltage across it meaning a one, or it doesn't mean a zero. It is in the nature of electricity that they can only be one voltage across the wire at a time and since each frame must be transmitted in its entirety without interruption, only one computer at a time can transmit a frame on the same stretch of cable. If at exactly the same instant, two computers attempt to transmit a frame, there'll be a collision and both frames will fail. Each computer must then wait a random amount of time, possibly only a tiny fraction of a second - the so called back off delay before attempting to transmit the failed frame again.

Frame collisions were common on an old-style LAN. The system for dealing with frame collisions is labeled as the CSMA/ **CD or Carrier Sense Multiple Access with Collision Detection,** fortunately this reaction happens very quickly. A typical Ethernet can carry up to 10 gigabits per second, that's a lot of frames! Modern wireless Ethernet uses a similar system but instead of cables, a wireless network uses high frequency radio waves. A wireless access point does the same job as the backbone cable, all frames are sent to this first and then they're relayed onwards.

Wi-Fi has a range of about a hundred meters, but this also depends on obstacles like walls, or hills, not to mention possible interference from devices like microwave ovens and cordless telephones. The closer you are to a Wi-Fi hotspot, the better.

To transmit Ethernet frames over Wi-Fi, the sender must first make its intention known to the wireless access point. If nothing else is transmitting, the wireless access point will let the sender know that it may continue. Frames are then relayed via the wireless access point to the intended recipient. A wireless network interface card can't transmit and receive at the same time, it is said to be half duplex. Since other computers may be too far away for direct communications, one computer doesn't necessarily know if another is attempting to transmit at the same time. Therefore, to avoid collisions which would corrupt Ethernet frames, everything must go through the wireless access point. This is called as the **CSMA/CA or Carrier Sense Multiple Access with Collision Avoidance** and it is the essence of how all Wi-Fi works today.

In case you are wondering why your neighbor's Wi-Fi doesn't interfere with yours, well it might. Normally each wireless access point operates within its own radio frequency range. When it sets itself up, it will choose a channel that seems quiet at the time and your wireless computers will tune in to this. Rather like when you tune in to a TV or radio station, a modern wireless access point can select one of twenty-three non-overlapping channels. So hopefully your neighbor's Wi-Fi will be operating in a different frequency range. Nevertheless, it is beneficial sometimes to change your Wi-Fi channel manually, especially in a crowded area. It should be said that wireless ethernet frames are normally encrypted so the data that you broadcast on the airwaves can't read even if it is deliberately intercepted.

LAN Topology

This refers to the placement or layout of the machines in a local area network. Specifically, how the computers are connected together. There are four main ways of connecting the computers in a LAN: the bus, star, ring, and mesh.

- **Bus Topology**

This type of structure involves a main backbone cable and the workstations are attached to this. The backbone cable can be up to a hundred meters long before an amplifier is needed to boost the signals. A typical bus LAN uses Ethernet technology and all of the workstations have an Ethernet network interface card (NIC) inside them. With any LAN, only one computer can transmit a packet of data at a time. Ethernet handles this by allowing any computer to attempt to put a signal on the cable at any time, then if there is a collision it is detected by the network interface card which waits a very brief casual number of time before giving another try to retransmit. The backbone cable has a terminator at either end, there is nothing more than electrical resistors designed to prevent signal echoes on the cable. The bus is the cheapest way to arrange a network because it uses the least amount of cable compared to other arrangements. It is easy to swap workstations or to add new ones without disrupting the rest of the LAN and if one workstation fails, the network will continue as long as there isn't a break in the main backbone cable.

- **Star Topology**

A star-shaped LAN, the computers and devices are all hooked up directly to a main device. Each workstation is independent of the rest so it's easy to add and remove workstations without disruptions. There may be a server at the center of the LAN or there may be a connecting box known as a hub, in which case the server will be connected to it just like the workstations. Although the name may suggest the topology's shape, the cable runs may vary in great length depending on how far away the workstations are from the center. For this reason, the star uses the most amount of cable compared to other arrangements and this makes it potentially the most expensive arrangement. Also, if the server or the central hub fails the whole LAN will go down.

- **Ring Topology**

This is more than just a way of connecting computers together. It's an alternative to Ethernet when it comes to controlling the way computers exchange packets of data. In a ring, an electrical signal called the token is passed from computer to computer at a very high speed and always in the same direction. The so-called token ring network interface card in each machine is responsible for propagating the token. When one computer wants to transmit a packet of data to another it takes control of the token. No other computer can send anything while it has possession of the token. The data is essentially attached to the token and sent on its way. The main benefit of a token ring network is that very fast transmission rates are possible because there are no collisions to be dealt with. However, because the network interface card of each computing devices in the token ring is responsible for maintaining the token if one machine fails, the whole network will fail. Adding new workstations involves shutting the whole network down. The ring is also potentially the most expensive arrangement because special token ring network interface cards cost more than ethernet cards.

- **Hubs**

In its simplest form, a hub is just a connecting box that simplifies the wiring of a local area network. By using a central hub with computers radiating out from the middle, you can create what looks like a star-shaped network. However, inside the hub there might be a ring or a bus. A hub can do more than just tidy up the wiring of a LAN. If it's also repeater, it will amplify signals on long stretches of cable. If a hub is a switch or a router, it can help to reduce the amount of unnecessary traffic on the LAN.

- **Mesh Network**

Wireless mesh networks are becoming more common. In the mesh, every device is connected to every other device. Either directly which is known as a full mesh or indirectly which is called partial mesh. This type of architecture has a lot of advantages, typically the administration tasks are decentralized. There's no controlling server, so there's no single point of failure because there are no cables involved. A wireless mesh is cheaper to set up particularly over a large area such as a whole city. Adding new nodes is easy, the network interface cards usually configure themselves when they detect nearby nodes. As the number of nodes increases, the network becomes even faster and more efficient. In a wireless mesh, data packets hop from node to node and will find the fastest route available.

Quick Notes:
- Topology refers to the layout of computers in a LAN
- Packets transmitted using Token, Ring, or Ethernet
- Layouts include bus, star, and ring
- Mesh is used for Wi-Fi networks
- Hubs can simplify wiring
- A large LAN might have several layouts

Standard Connectors

Connectors are very similar whether it is a loopback cable, whether it is a rollover cable, whether it is an ethernet straight through or crossover; the connectors themselves look exactly the same to our eyes, the only difference is how it is wired inside of that jacket.

- RJ- 11 Connector

The letters RJ means registered jack; this is a four-wired connector used mainly to connect telephone equipment. As far as computer networking is concerned, it is used to hook up computers to local area network via the computer's modem. The rj-11 locks itself in place by a hinge-locking tab and it resembles the rj-45 but is considerably smaller in size.

- RJ-45 Connector

By far, the rj-45 is the most common connector. This is an eight-wired connector that is used to connect computers to local area networks. It is used with twisted pair cabling. Like the rj-11, it locks itself in place by a hinge-locking tab.

- RJ-48c Connector

This connector looks similar to rj-45. The difference between the two, the rj-48c is used with shielded twisted pair instead of unshielded twisted pair. It is primary used with T1 lines and it is also wired differently than the rj-45.

- UTP Coupler

This is used to connect UTP cables with rj-45 connectors to each other. This is typically used when running a longer cable is either not an option or not available. The user needs to hook the end of the cable into the coupler and then add another cable on the other side. By doing so, it would successfully extend the existing UTP cables.

- BNC Connector

This belongs to a standard category of RF connector that is utilized in coaxial cables. The letters BNC stands for Bayonet Neill–Concelman. It is used for both analog and digital video transmissions as well as audio.

- BNC Coupler

This is used to connect two coaxial cables with BNC connectors attached to them. This particular coupler is a BNC female to female coupler.

- Fiber Coupler

If two fiber connectors are needed to be joined together then a fiber coupler is required to complete the task. This coupler is used to join two of the same fiber optic connectors. The two connectors have to be the same type, this is not to be confused with a fiber adapter which is used for joining two different connectors together such as an SC to an ST and so on.

- F-Type Connector

This is a threaded connector that is typically used with coaxial cables. These are primarily used by cable providers to attach cable modems. The F-Type tightens by an attached nut.

USB Connector

- Universal Serial Bus or USB connector is very common in both desktops and laptops. Majority of computer manufacturers make wireless cards that can be plugged to a usb port. The usb has two different connector types: Type A and Type B.

- IEEE 1394

This connector is also known as the firewire, it can be recognized with its D-shaped connector. This type of connection is also widely common in desktops. Laptops and even tablets and some smartphones. It is widely associated with peripheral devices such as digital cameras, multimedia devices, videos, and printers rather than being used in network connections.

- MT-RJ Connector

This is designated for the fiber optic connection. MT-RJ stands for Mechanical Transfer Registered Jack. It is a fiber optic cable connector and it uses a latched push-pull connector. It has a small-form factor built for high - packed density.

- ST Connector

A straight tip connector uses a half-twist bayonet type of lock. This is commonly used in a single mode fiber optic cable.

- LC (Connector)

The local connector is also used as a fiber optic connector. It uses jack that is similar to rj-45. This is commonly used as a connector for cables between floors in a building.

- SC (Connector)

The standard connector uses a push - pull connector that is similar to audio and video plugs. Like the LC connector, this is also commonly used between floors in a building

- RS-232 Connector

The term Serial refers to sending data, one bit at a time. Serial cables are the types of cables that carries serial data transmission. The most common form of serial cables is using the standard RS-232 Connector which has the common "D" connector, such as the DB-9 and DB-25.

Network Cable Standards

There are specific cables needed to be used for local area networks (LAN), these are the twisted cables or the ethernet cables that computer users can find as a connection is established from the computer to the router or modem in order to obtain internet access. One end of the cable plugs into the computer's network interface card (NIC) while the other end is connected to the network port of the router switch or modem depending upon what is being used in the network.

Ethernet twisted pair cables come in two different types; the first type is the Unshielded Twisted Pair – is frequently described as the most regular type of cable that is used more recently. This type is consisting of four pairs of wires that are color coded then twisted around within itself, the wires are twisted to prevent electromagnetic interference or crosstalk. This cable can be commonly found in most people's homes or businesses. The second type is the Shielded Twisted Pair (STP). The STP is highly similar to the unshielded twisted-pair except that it has a foil shield that covers the wires. This shielding adds an extra layer of protection against electromagnetic interference leaking into and out of the cable.

This type of cable is mainly used for industrial purposes and not so much in homes or businesses.

In some cases where the network administrator or the user prefers to make their own custom cables for the network, typically a bulk roll of twisted pair cable can be purchased from a store. From there, it can be wired correctly by attaching rj45 connectors to each end. To achieve this, the protective shielding at the end of each network cable needs to be removed to expose the wire. This is done by using a cable stripper, the cable is inserted into the cable stripper and then the outer sheathing is removed to expose the wires and then the cable needs to be inserted into a wire crimper to attach a rj45 connector. It is important to note that the wires in the cable have to arranged in a certain order and that order will be different depending upon the purpose of the cable.

Common types of twisted pair cables:
- Straight Patch Cable
- Crossover Cable

When it comes to the wiring order of these twisted pair cables, there are two different standards that are used within the industry: one is the 568A and the other standard is 568B.

The orders are based on the color of the wires.

568A

- White - Green
- Green
- White - Orange
- Blue
- White - Blue
- Orange
- White - Brown
- Brown

568B:

- White - Orange
- Orange
- White - Green
- Blue
- White - Blue
- Green
- White - Brown
- Brown

*The main difference among the A and the B standards is the green wires are swapped with the orange. It doesn't really matter which standard is used, both standards do the same thing. Here in the United States, most people use the B standard.

Whether the A or the B wiring standard is chosen, if both ends of the cable are wired using the same standard, then this is known as a Straight Cable which is also known as a Patch Cable. A straight cable allows signal to pass through from end to end. This is the most common type of cable that is utilized in the local area networks. A straight cable manages to connect computers to hubs, switches, routers or modems. In other words, it is used to connect dissimilar devices together, making it the most common cable that is being used on LANs.

A Crossover Cable is also used on local area networks, but it is not as common as a straight cable. A crossover cable is created when both ends of a cable are wired using the two different standards. For example: one end is wired using the A standard and the other end is wired using the B standard. Crossover cables are used to connect two similar devices together. A common scenario is between two computers, crossover cables are utilized to attach devices directly to each other beyond the use of a hub or a switch. It is capable to be utilized for connection between hubs to hubs, or switches to switches.

There are also the categories of twisted cables. These are Cat 3, Cat 4, Cat 5, Cat 6, and Cat 7. The difference between these categories is the maximum speed they can handle without having crosstalk or interference. The numbers of the category represent the tightness of the twist that are applied to the wires. The speed ranges from the lowest category which is 3 at 10 megabits per second and all the way to Cat 6a and Cat 7 which has speeds of 10 gigabits per second. Most networks of today would use at least Cat 5e on their networks because most networks would be running at least at gigabit speeds. Cat 3 and Cat 5 are slower than gigabit and are pretty much obsolete today. In case the user is at a network speed that is running slower, Cat 7 can still be used because it is backward compatible. The Cat 7 is actually a shielded twisted-pair version of Cat 6a.

CATEGORY	SPEED	
CATEGORY 3	10 Mbps	Currently obsolete
CATEGORY 5	100 Mbps	Currently obsolete
CATEGORY 5e	1 Gbps	Enhanced
CATEGORY 6	1 Gbps	10 Gbps (cable length under 100 meters)
CATEGORY 6a	10 Gbps	Augmented
CATEGORY 7	10 Gbps	Added shielding to the wires
CATEGORY 8	40 Gbps	Distance up to 30 meters

The latest version is Cat 8. It is the ultimate copper cable; it is also a shielded twisted-pair cable which has a delivery speed of up to 40 gigabits per second up to a distance of 30 meters. In comparison, this is 4 times faster than the Cat 6a or Cat 7.

Chapter 4: Firewall

Firewall

A firewall is a procedure in place that has been engineered to restrict unwarranted access from coming into a private network by monitoring the information that arrives from the internet. It stops unwelcomed traffic while it allows valid traffic. A firewall's purpose is to create a safety barrier between a private network and the public internet, because on the internet there's always going to be hackers and malicious traffic that may try to penetrate into a private network to cause harm. A firewall if the primary component on a network to prevent this.

A firewall is especially important to any organization that has a lot of computers and servers in them. It is unideal to have all those devices accessible to everyone on the internet where a hacker can come in and totally disrupt that organization.

Imagine how a firewall works in a building structure, it is very similar to how firewall's used in computer networks work. In fact, this is where the word "firewall" came from. A firewall in a building structure provides a barrier so that in the event of an actual fire, on either side of a building, the firewall is there to keep the fire contained and to keep it from spreading over to the other side. The firewall, in concept, is there to keep the fire from destroying the entire building. If a firewall is not present to contain the flames, it is extremely easy and fast to spread the fire to the entire building structure. A network firewall works in a similar way. It stops harmful activities before it can spread into the other of the firewall and cause harm to a private network.

In today's high-tech world, a firewall is essential to every home and especially in a business or an organization to keep their network safe.

A firewall works by filtering the incoming data and determines by its rules if it is allowed to enter a network. These rules are also known as an Access Control List. These rules are customizable and are determined by the network administrator. The administrator decides not only what can enter a network but also what can leave a network. These rules either allows or denies permission.

Firewall rules can be based on:
- IP Addresses
- Domain names
- Protocols
- Programs
- Ports
- Keywords

Firewalls come in different types. One type is Host-based Firewall - this is a software firewall. This is the kind that is installed on a computer and it protects that computer only and nothing else.

Another type of firewall is called Network-based Firewall. This is a conjunction between a hardware together with software and it operates at the network layer. It is placed between a private network and the public internet. Unlike host-based firewall, where it can only protect the computer where it is installed, a network-based protects the entire network and it does this through management rules that are applied to the entire network. Any harmful activity can be stopped before it reaches the computers. Network-based firewalls can be a standalone product which is mainly used by large organizations, it can also be a built-in as a component of a router which is what a lot of smaller organizations rely on. Another way is to have it deployed in a service provider's cloud infrastructure.

A lot of organizations tend to use both network-based and host-based firewalls, this method provides a multi-layer protection.

DMZ (Demilitarized Zone)

To enhance the security of an organization, another approach is being used - seclusion or separation; this method is called

DMZ. Digital devices like servers and computers sit on the contrasting ends of a firewall. The concept is almost like creating two separate networks. The next logical question is, "Why would a user want this? How does the DMZ accomplish this, if it really can?"

For example: In a company's computer network, there could be a web server and an email server. Typically, these kinds of servers sit behind a network's firewall, these servers are inside the company' private network. This would mean that the company is somehow letting in people from untrusted network (the internet), given access behind the company's firewall and into the company's private network where the servers are.

The example set up could cause a security concern because as people are accessing these servers, hackers could use the same opportunity and use as an opening to cause havoc in a computer network. Remember at this point, outsiders have already got past the firewall because servers are behind the firewall. Hackers can try and access other sensitive data from other devices that are also behind the firewall, such as a database server where sensitive data is kept, or hacker may even try to plant a virus in the network.

What if a company or any network administrator put the public access to web and email servers outside the network's internal firewall and put it on the opposite side of the firewall?

The servers would still be located within the same building and need not be physically removed, but it would be configured to be on the other side of the firewall.

In this set up, whenever people access the servers from the internet, they are not going to be accessing them behind the network's internal firewall - where most of the sensitive information are kept, the servers are now out in front facing the internet and fully exposed.

This is exactly what DMZ is.

DMZ is sometimes referred to as the Perimeter Network. As a perimeter network, it acts like a screened network to detect any malicious activity before it can get pass the firewall and into the internal network. The DMZ divides the network into two parts: by taking the devices from inside the firewall and then putting it outside the firewall. Some networks that uses DMZ only uses one firewall, however larger companies that have more sensitive data at stake tend to use at least two firewalls to secure its network. Extra firewall will be added and then be put in front of a DMZ, the second firewall adds an extra layer of protection to ensure that only legitimate traffic can access the DMZ. This more secure setup also makes it harder for would - be hackers to penetrate into the network because they have to go through two different firewalls.

There is also a DMZ that can be configured for home - use. This can be done using a standard router. In the advanced settings of the router's configuration page, there is typically a section there that talks about setting up a DMZ. This setup is not entirely a true DMZ but rather it is just setting up a DMZ host. Creating a DMZ in a home-based router appoints a device as a DMZ host and will send and push all the ports to that device.

A common use of a DMZ for a home setup is to put it with gaming consoles such as an Xbox or PlayStation and configuring it as a DMZ host. This is typically done because a lot of these gaming consoles are often used for online gaming. Most gamers do not want any interference that could happen from a firewall, so it is unlikely that gamers would like to change the settings of any kind that would have something to do with port forwarding configuration. Gamers could just go into the DMZ settings in the router and put in the gaming console's IP address as the DMZ.

It is very important to note that the device in the DMZ is set with a static IP address rather than a dynamic IP address.

In summary: In the real world, the DMZ is an area where the military is forbidden. In the computing world, DMZ is where the firewall protection is forbidden.

Chapter 5: Network Components

Hub, Switch, Router and Modems

These apparatuses are similar in concept but there is a contrast in the way they manage data.

Hub

The function of a hub is to hook up all of the network devices together on an internal network, it is a gear that has several ports that can allow ethernet connections from network devices. A hub is not regarded to be intelligent. It does not have the ability to filter any data. The hub also does not have the intelligence to direct where the data should be sent to. The lone element the hub knows is whenever a device is attached to its port, when a data packet reaches one of the ports, it is duplicated to all other ports.

In by doing so, data packets are visible to all the devices on that hub.

A data packet comes in to one port, then the hub will just rebroadcast that data to each of the ports that has a device attached to it.

In a scenario where four computers all belong to the same network, which are also connected to the same hub: if computer A wanted to communicate with computer B, then computers C and D would still receive the data even though the data was not intended for them.

Aside from the security concerns this setup may have constructed, it also generates avoidable traffic on the network which as a result, misuse the bandwidth.

Switch

A switch is immensely comparable to a hub. It is device that has a number of ports that allows ethernet connections from network devices. In comparison with a hub, a switch is intelligent. A switch has the ability to determine the physical addresses of the digital equipment that are attached to it and save these information - the physical addresses called MAC address in its data bank. When a data packet is dispatched to a switch, it is only routed to the planned destination port.

In a scenario where in a private network, there are four computers that are attached to the same hub: if computer D wanted to communicate with computer C, then the switch will seek the information at its data bank of MAC addresses and matching ports and hand over the data to the appropriate port. The data packet would only be passed to the computer C, its intended destination. Computers B and A would not be affected by that instance of communication.

Because of its efficiency, most users and network administrators favor switches than the hubs because of its capacity to reduce unnecessary traffic on the network.

Quick Notes:

- Hubs and switches are utilized to swap data within a LAN
- These devices are not meant to send and receive data outside their own network, for example – the internet
- To exchange or route data outside their own network to another network, i.e., the internet, a device needs to be able to read IP addresses.
- Hubs and switches do not have the ability to scan and interpret IP addresses, only switches can read MAC addresses

Router

A router does correctly what its name suggests, it is a device that directs or forwards data from a network to another network depending on their IP addresses. When a data packet has arrived from the router, the device's job is to inspect the data's IP address and figure out if the packet was intended for its own network or if it is designated to be sent to another network. If the router has concluded that the data packet is originally directed for its own network, it acquires the data. If the packet is determined not to be directed for its own network, the router dispatches it to separate network. A router can be described accurately as a network's gateway.

Quick Notes:
- Hubs and switches are employed to build networks
- Routers are designed to affix networks

What is the difference between a modem and a router?

Others may probably have the impression that modem and a router are equivalent of each other, they are not. These two devices are distinctive with each having independent roles on a network.

If internet is required inside an establishment, a user needs to have a modem. A modem is responsible in delivering the internet into an establishment. A modem establishes and maintains a devoted connection to your internet service provider (ISP) to grant connection to the internet.

The logic why a modem is needed is - as a result of having a couple of types of signals that are utilized on a computer and when the devices are connected to the internet. A computer only has the ability to interpret digital signals, although these signals that are out on the internet are classified to be as analog.

In the process of analog data coming in from the internet, the modem demodulates the arriving analog signals and transcribes it as digital signals so that a computer can read it.

A modem also modulates outgoing digital signals from a computer into an analog signal as it goes out on the internet.

The context behind the word modem is a device that is designed as a modulator and demodulator - which precisely how a modem operates. It modulates the data that are on its way out from a computer and demodulates incoming or arriving data from the internet.

There are routers that are being utilized in businesses and larger institutions, and there are smaller routers that are utilized in homes and startup businesses - but essentially these types do the same thing.

In a single computer setup, a user doesn't need a router to access the internet. The user can directly plug the network cable of the computer into the modem and then end user will be able to access the internet. However, in a computer networking set up - like in most homes and businesses, multiple devices need to have access and be connected to the internet and that is where a router is needed.

Types of Modems

Some of the common types are cable and DSL modems. This rests upon what type of internet that is being used, the accurate type of modem is required.

Cable modems are directed and attached to a home or business by means of a coaxial cable. This type of connection - cable internet, is typically provided by the same company that provides you with cable television.

DSL modems are connected using a typical phone line.

For home and small business, ISPs may provide a modem device that acts as combination of router and a modem. It is a modem with an incorporated wireless router in a single physical device.

Mesh Wi-Fi System

The most preferred way of connecting to the internet by many is through wireless connection, it gives the users flexibility to move around and still be connected to the network without the limitations that wired connection might have.

In some instances where a few areas or spots within a structure gets a weaker Wi-Fi signal, it can be described as "spotty". For example, there might be some areas in a house or office where the signal is weak, or it may be totally unavailable. There are several reasons why spotty signal might incur - as we have discussed in the Wi-Fi section of this book, or just the placement of the Wi-Fi router may also affect the way the signal strength in some areas can be.

To remedy this problem, a lot of times people would buy just a Wi-Fi extender to help and extend the Wi-Fi signal. Even though Wi-Fi extenders do work, some issues may occur since Wi-Fi extenders create its own Wi-Fi network that has its own separate SSID. In this case, the user would have to connect to the Wi-Fi where the signal is stronger - whether from the router or to the Wi-Fi extender's network, depending on where the user is at within a structure.

Another option to expand Wi-Fi signal within a structure is by using a Mesh Wi-Fi System. It is the latest technology as an answer to the problems of weak or dead spot issues with Wi-Fi.

A mesh Wi-Fi is a group of routers or Wi-Fi points that are placed in different locations inside an infrastructure. It provides a blanket of Wi-Fi coverage within a closed area like a home or small office. It does the job of eliminating weak Wi-Fi signals.

A good feature of this technology is that the Wi-Fi points communicate with each other wireless to create one large Wi-Fi network. There are no cables involved when Wi-Fi points are communicating with each other which makes the placement of the Wi-Fi points that much easier.

A sample setup using mesh Wi-Fi: A modem - router that brings the internet into the home or office, then attach one of the mesh Wi-Fi points to the modem - router using an ethernet cable and the other Wi-Fi points can be placed around the infrastructure as needed. Once the physical setup is complete, the Wi-Fi points will communicate or talk to each other to create a seamless internet connection that covers the entire house or small office for all of the wireless devices to connect to. This system creates a large Wi-Fi network, each Wi-Fi point is not creating its own Wi-Fi network with SSID like an extender would be like.

A device that is connected to the network will seamlessly disconnect from a Wi-Fi point and then reconnect to another Wi-Fi point.

Quick Notes:

- How hubs and switches relate to modems and modem-routers?
  - Most routers will have an in-built switch integrated to it, if this is the case, it is not a requirement to have a switch if you network has a router with a switch built into it.
- A possible reason why you would require to add a switch despite having a router with a built-in switch, is if you needed more wired connections for your devices and all of the ports in your router have been exhausted. A switch can be connected to the router, then additional devices can be connected to the network through the switch.

Chapter 6: Wireless Technology

Wireless network connects computers and other digital devices through the air via radio waves. Wireless networks are commonly called as Wireless Local Area Networks (WLAN), another term that is widely used is "Wi-Fi".

Wireless networks can be structured in various ways; however, the basic components remain the same.

Access Point (AP) - this is the "heart" of the network and the links connect it to the nodes. This is the wireless router; it provides access to the internet and other to the other computers within the network. Typically, a router is hardwired to a modem or in some cases a multipurpose device like the modem - router can be used. Typically, the internet access is going through ethernet wires. From this moment on, the network becomes wireless.

Links

These are radio waves instead of instead of wires, it uses one or two bands of spectrum; 2.4GHz or 5 GHz. The earlier band is shared with microwaves, baby monitors, garage door openers, and many other non Wi-Fi devices - all of which can cause interference to the network. The 2.4 GHz has a longer range compared to 5 GHz spectrum; however, the latter is extremely less crowded but since it does have a shorter range to extend its range capacity, it might require multiple access points as needed

Nodes

These are the computers or workstations and all other digital devices that can be connected to the Wi-Fi. Laptops and desktops have information cards that receive and send data through radio waves, the mobile devices like a smartphone or a tablet are like two-way radios in the sense that they receive and transmit radio waves to link to the access points

How is a device recognized by wireless network?

A custom code is being used by the computer, this the Transmission Control Protocol / Internet Protocol. The TCP follows rules to create and assemble packets of information and the IP sends and receives these data. An IP address is assigned to a computer or every digital device while it in the network.

What is the difference between 2.4 GHz and 5 GHz Wi-Fi Routers?

The technology of today lets us have wider options when it comes to devices. This is also true for Wireless Networks. You might have noticed some Wi-Fi routers that have both 2.4GHz and 5 GHz frequency bands.

A frequency band is how wireless data is transmitted between devices. These bands are radio waves that carry the data and these bands are either 2.4GHz and 5 GHz. Previously, most Wi-Fi routers will only transmit one of these bands which is the 2.4 band since it is the most common frequency, and these are called Single Band Routers. Newer routers that can transmit both bands are referred to as Dual Band Wi-Fi routers.

At this point we have learned how the 2.4 GHz is the standard band, however it is not just a standard band that is being used in Wi-Fi routers. It is also the standard band that is utilized in a lot of other devices like microwave ovens and cordless phones, Bluetooth devices, wireless cameras, just to name a few. This became a problem because the fact that so many other devices use the 2.4 band the signal tend to become overcrowded and was causing a lot of interference with Wi-Fi signals. Whenever this happens, it slows down the Wi-Fi network speed and sometimes can cause to disrupt or lose connection to the Wi-Fi router.

The 5 GHz band was added to try to resolve the overcrowding issue of the previous band. The newer band is not as commonly used as the 2.4 so it is used by fewer devices, as a result there is minimal to no interference in the signal. Using the 5 GHz would relieve the problem related to slow network speeds and connection drops that is typically caused by interference from other devices.

Another reason why the 2.4 band is more vulnerable to interference is because of the difference in wireless channels. A wireless channel is a way to fine-tune and alter a frequency. Sometimes it is needed to change the channel in the router whenever high-interference is being experienced within a channel. The 2.4 GHz band has 11 channels to choose from (1,2,3,4,5,6,7,8,9,10,11); but of these 11 channels only three are non-overlapping (channels 1, 3, and 11). Basically, in this band there are only 3 solid channels to choose from. The 5Ghz band has more channels, it has 25 non-overlapping channels.

Another difference between the two are the speed and range that it can cover. The 2.4 GHz band transmits data at a slower speed than the 5 GHz, but it does have a broader dimension covered. The 5GHz band has the ability to broadcast data at a faster speed but it has a shorter range because it has higher frequency, and as the frequency gets higher it gets difficult for it to pass through or penetrate solid objects such as floors and walls in a building.

Overview:

2.4 GHz

- Advantages:
  - Farther range
  - Can penetrate solid objects
- Disadvantages
- Vulnerable to interference
- Slower speed

5GHz

- Advantages:
- Higher transfer speed
- Less vulnerable to interference

- Disadvantages
- Shorter range
- Harder time penetrating solid objects

802.11 Channel Access

RF is an open shared medium, since we operate in a license-free space with 802.11 such as 2.4 GHz, portions of the 5 GHz all the way down to 50 GHz for some of the television whitespace and all the way up to 60 GHz with 802.11a/d or Multi-Gigabit (DMG) devices physical layers. There is more frequency space that we use today than ever with 802.11, however the one thing they all share in common is that they are open shared medium. Meaning, multiple devices on the same channel must share access and the device cannot detect what is happening somewhere else. There is no way for a transmitting station to know as it is sending information that the receiving station does not have interference or some other factor that might be impacting it there. We utilize a special type of communication in 802.11 networks like Acknowledgement Frames to acknowledge the receipt of information. An algorithm is needed to assist in the prevention of collisions.

Devices should be able to detect signal at the lowest modulation rate used within the channel. This is a requirement of 802.11 channel access; it needs to be able to see that signal at the lowest possible data rate. The lowest data rate is the one that you can demodulate at the greatest distance. If something is sent at a low data rate even at a distance, you should be able to decode or demodulate that data. This is the primary key to proper wireless LAN shared access, the need to be able to detect signal at the lowest modulation rate.

Quick Notes:
- RF is an open medium
- Multiple devices in the same channel must share access
- Devices cannot detect what is happening in other locations

- An algorithm is needed to assist in the prevention of collisions (Collision Avoidance)
- Devices should be able to detect signals at the lowest modulation rate within the channel
- This is the primary key to proper WLAN shared access

The wireless technology has helped us to transfer data from one device to another without using wires or cables. Using this technology, we can now establish a network is more flexible, intangible and has ease of access.

The use of smartphones or tablets or any other wireless devices that support Wi-Fi, wireless networking has allowed us to move around an area without hesitation since the device is still connected to the network.

In wires connection, data passes through cables whereas in wireless connection the data is passing through radio frequency (RF) signal.

The frequency of the Radio Frequency or RF signals ranges from 30kHz to 300 GHz, it falls under the category of EM waves or electromagnetic waves. A light is a good example of an electromagnetic wave; however, we can see a light as it passes through, RF signal on the other hand is completely not visible to us.

In radios, FM radio stations uses RF signal to broadcast signals. The frequency signal being used is frequently the same as the station name, for example KIIS-FM 102.7 (the 102.7 in the station name is the frequency it uses).

RF Signal range: 30kHz to 300 GHz

Types of Wireless Network

- Wireless LAN
- Wireless MAN
- Wireless WAN
- Wireless PAN

Wireless LAN (Local Area Network)

This is a network where there are two or more computers or devices connected to the network and it only covers a limited area, for example a home or small business. The NIC is sed in this type of network, we often call this the Peer-to-Peer Network (P2P). Another form of this is an ad-hoc network which is used in temporary manner.

Unlike using switch in a wired network, in the WLAN setup we use a device called an access point. This is a central device from which the RF signal is being generated. WLAN which uses access point are called Basic Service Set (BSS), it acts as the coordinator between different devices within the network.

Wi-Fi

RF signal Frequency: 2.4 GHz or 5 GHz

Range: 100 meters

Wi-Fi products are certified and tested by the Wi-Fi Alliance

Wireless MAN (Wireless Metropolitan Area Network)

Collected unit of many WLANs located at various places

Uses WIMAX technology (Worldwide Interoperability for Microwave Access) which is controlled by WiMAX Forum

Maximum Speed: 1 Gbits/ sec

IEEE 802.16 Standard

WWAN (Wireless Wide Area Network)

This is an extensive network that has been distributed across an immense amount of space. It connects cities together. Mobile phones use WWAN to make communication possible.

The technology in WWAN are subdivided in generations: 2G, 3G, and 4G

Most analog devices are utilizing this technology

- Examples of 2g
- General Packet Radio Service (GPRS)
- Enhanced Data rates for GSM Evolution (EDGE)

- Examples of 3G (third generation technologies)
- Code Division Multiple Access (CDMA)
- Universal Mobile Telecommunication System (UMTS)

- High Speed Packet Access (HSPA)
- Evolved High Speed Packet Access (HSPA+)

- 4G (High Speed Network accessibility can be achieved with this technology)
- Long Term Evolution (LTE)
- Voice Over Long-Term Evolution (VoLTE)

Time Evolution

In 1G in the 2980s, the only single voice was going from one device to another device. The analog protocol was being utilized during this period. In mid 1980s 2G network has introduced, with it came voice and text capabilities. Both voice and text messages are going from one device to another device with the use of digital standards. The speed from 1G (2.4 kbps) has increased when 2G was invented (16 kbps). In 2003, 3G has evolved from voice and text, with now including data. It uses the multimedia technologies and has a speed of up to 2 Mb per second. In 2009 4G was introduced to the market, this technology allows voice to go through data. IP protocol is utilized, and the speed can reach up to 100 Mb per second. 5G technology is the next one to hit the market soon, it will have more bandwidth mobility which a key factor for it would be to succeed.

WPAN (Wireless Personal Area Network)

This kind of network is used smaller distance

Technologies that are mostly used for WPAN are Bluetooth and Infrared Data Association

Bluetooth

- Uses ISM band of 2.4 GHz
- Speed of up to 721Kbps
- Range goes anywhere between 10 to 100 meters

If you are using Bluetooth technology, let's say in your headset or keyboard or speakers and it is connected to your smartphone or tablet, this is an example of a personal wireless area network

VLAN (Virtual Local Area Network)

A VLAN is a local area network where the computers, servers, and other network devices are logically connected regardless of their physical location. This means, even if the devices connected to the network are scattered in different places, it would not matter because a VLAN can logically group these devices into separate virtual networks.

The purposes of a VLAN

- Improved security
- Traffic management
- Make a network simpler

A VLAN capable switch can logically create several virtual networks to separate network broadcast traffic. This can be done by designating specific ports on the switch and assigning those ports to a specific VLAN.

VLAN helps with traffic management because as a local area network grows and more network devices are added, the frequency of the broadcast will also increase, and the network will get heavily congested with data. By creating VLANs, it will divide up the network into smaller broadcast domains, it will help alleviate the broadcast traffic

Security Options

Data can be easily hacked in Wireless Network without using proper security protocols. RF signals can be intercepted by other antennas.

IEEE Standards

The acronym stands for Institute of Electrical and Electronics Engineers.

Since there are various types of technology available for wireless networks, IEEE was established to determine standards for functioning of wireless networks.

Most networking standards are designed by 802 LAN/MAN Standards Committee.

IEEE Wireless Standards

- The first Wireless LAN was successfully made in 1997
- IEEE 802.11 Standard was designed because of WLAN
- Frequency used: 2.4 GHz
- Maximum Speed: 2Mbps
- This is now referred to as 802.11 Legacy

802.11a

Frequency: 5 GHz

Maximum Speed: 54 Mbps

802.11b

Frequency: 2.4 GHz

Maximum Speed: 11 Mbps

These standards were introduced in the same year in the late 1990s

802.11g

Frequency: 2.4 GHz

Maximum Speed: 54 Mbps

Introduced in 2003

802.11n

Frequency: 2.4 GHz and 5 GHz

Maximum Speed: 300 Mbps

Usual drawbacks of Wireless Networking

- RF signal strength gets weaker as the distance increases
- The signal may be affected by structures like concrete walls, big objects, and other similar items
- Unsecured signal can be easily targeted for hacking and can be intercepted

Chapter 7: OSI Reference Model

OSI Model or Open System Interconnection Model

OSI model defines and is used to understand how data is transferred from one computer to another in a computer network in the most basic form two computers connected to each other with a LAN cable and connectors sharing data with the help of network interface card forms a network but if one computer is based using Microsoft Windows and the other computer has Mac OS installed, then how are these two computers are going to communicate with each other in order to successful communication between computers or networks or different architectures seven layers OSI models or Open System Interconnection Model was introduced by the International Organization for Standardization or ISO in 1984 containing:

- Application Layer
- Presentation Layer
- Session Layer
- Transport Layer
- Network Layer
- Data Link Layer
- Physical Layer

Each layer is a package of protocols, independent of each other.

For example, in Application Layer, it does not mean it includes computer applications like Chrome, Firefox, or similar web browsers, but it includes application layer protocols that are needed to make these applications work correctly in the network or on the Internet.

Application Layer:

Used by network applications. Network Application means, computer applications that utilize the internet, like web browsers, Microsoft Outlook, Skype just to name a few.

The web browser is a network application running in your computer, but it uses application layer protocols like HTTP or HTTPS to do web surfing. Not only web browsing but all network applications are dependent on application layer protocols to function. There are dozens of application layer protocols aside from HTTP and HTTPS (FTP, NFS, FMTP, DHCP, SNMP, TELNET, POP3, IRC, NNTP) that enable various functions at this layer all these protocols collectively are the basis for various network services like file transfer, web surfing, emails, virtual terminal, etc.

- File transfer is done with the help of FTP protocol
- Web surfing is done with HTTP or HTTPS
- Emails utilizes SMTP

- For virtual terminal, telnet is used

Application layer provides services for network applications with the help of protocols to perform user activities

Presentation Layer

The presentation layer receives data coming from the application layer. This data is in the form of characters and numbers. Presentation layer converts these characters to machine-understandable binary format

For example: Conversion of ASCII ---> EBCDIC this function of the presentation layer is called translation. Before data is transmitted, the presentation layer reduces the number of bits that are used to represent the original data. this bit reduction process is called data compression and the results can be "lossy" or "lossless". Data compression reduces the amount of space used to store the original file as the size of the file is reduced it can be received at the destination in very little time, data transmission can be done faster thus data compression is helpful in real-time video and audio streaming. To maintain the integrity of the data before transmission, data is encrypted. Encryption enhances the security of sensitive data. At the sender side, data is encrypted and at the receiver side, the data is decrypted. SSL or Secure Sockets Layer protocol is used in the presentation layer for encryption and decryption. The presentation layer performs three basic functions: translation, compression, and encryption/decryption.

Session Layer

Suppose, you have planned for a party, you have hired a few helpers ensuring that each activity runs smoothly. Helpers will help you in setting up, assist in cleaning, and then closing the party. It is similar to the session layer. In this part of the process, this layer helps in setting up and managing connections, enabling sending and receiving of data followed by termination of connections or sessions. Like when you hired some helpers for a party, session layer too has its own helpers called APIs or Application Programming Interfaces, NETBIOS (network basic input/output system) is an example of APIs which allows applications on separate computers to talk with each other just before a session or a connection is established with the server. The server performs a function called authentication. Authentication is the process of verifying who you are. For this process, the server uses a username and a password, once this information is entered, it is masked a session, or a connection is established between your computer and the server. After authenticating the user authorization is checked. Authorization is the process used by a server to determine if you have permission to access a file, if not you will typically get a message saying, "you are not authorized to access this page". Both of these functions for authentication and authorization are performed by the session layer.

The session layer keeps track of the files that are being downloaded. For example, a web page contains text and images, this information is stored as separate files on the webserver. When you request a website in your web browser, your web browser offers a separate session to the webserver to download each of these text and image files separately these files are received in the form of data packets. The session layer keeps a track of which data packet belongs to which file either text file or image file and tracks where the received data packet goes, for this example it goes to the browser that is session layer helps in session management so.

The session layer helps in session management, authentication, and authorization. Your web browser performs all functions of the session, presentation, and application layer.

Transport Layer

The transport layer controls the reliability of communication through segmentation, flow control, and error control. In segmentation, data received that came from the session layer is divided into small data units called segments. Each segment contains a source, a destination a port number and a sequence number. A port number helps to direct each segment to the correct application. The sequence number helps to reassemble segments in the correct order to form the correct message at the receiver. Inflow control, the transport layer controls the amount of data being transmitted. For example, our smartphone is connected to a server, supposed a server can broadcast data maximum at 100 Mbps and our smartphone can process data at a maximum of 10 Mbps. Now, if we download a file from the server, but the server starts sending data at 50 Mbps, which is a lot higher than the rate of our smartphone can process. With the help of the transport layer, a smartphone can tell the server to slow down the data transmission rate up to 10 Mbps so no data gets lost. Similarly, is a server is sending data at 5 Mbps, a smartphone can request the server to increase the data transmission rate to 10 Mbps to maintain system performance.

The transport layer also helps in error control. If some data does not arrive at the destination, the transport layer uses automatic repeat request schemes to rebroadcast the missing or damaged data. A group of bits called checksum is added to each segment by the transport layer to find out the received can update segment. Protocols of the transport layer are the TCP and UDP (transmission control protocol and user datagram protocol). Transport layer performs two types of services: connection-oriented transmission and connectionless transmission. Connection-oriented transmission is done via TCP while Connectionless Transmission is done via UDP. UDP is faster than TCP because it does not provide any feedback whether data was really delivered. Whereas TCP provides feedback. Therefore, lost data can be retransmitted in TCP. UDP is used where it does not matter whether we have received all data. For example, online streaming movies, songs, games, voice over IP (VOIP), TFTP, DNS, etc. On the other hand, TCP is used were full data delivery is a must. For example, world wide web, email, FTP, etc. Transport layer is involved in segmentation, flow control, error control, connection oriented, and connectionless transmission. Transport layer passes data segments through the network layer.

Network Layer

Network layer works for the transmission of the received data segments from one computer to another located in different networks. Data units in the network layer are called packets. It is the layer where routers reside.

The function of network layer are logical addressing routing and path determination. IP addressing done in network layer is called logical addressing. Each computer in a network needs to have a distinct IP address. Network layer assigns sender and receiver's IP address to each segment to form an IP packet. IP addresses are assigned to ensure that each data packet can reach the correct destination. The routing is a method of moving data packet from source to destination and it is based on the logical address format of IPV4 or IPV6. Suppose computer A is connected to network one and computer B is connected to network two. From computer B we have requested to access Facebook or communication and now there is a reply from Facebook server for them to be in the form of packets. This packet needs to be delivered to computer B only. Since in a network, each device has a unique IP address, so these both computers will be having a unique IP address as well. Network layer of the Facebook server has already added sender and receiver's IP address in the packet. Suppose mask used is 225.225.225.0, this mask tells that the first 3 combination represents network while the last combination represents host or computer B so based on IP address format received data packet will move first to network 2 and then to computer B. So, based on IP address and mask routing decisions are made in a computer network. Now path determination. A computer can be connected to internet server for a computer in a number of ways. Choosing the best possible path for data delivery from source to destination is called Path Determination. Layer C devices uses protocols such as Open Shortest Path First (OSPF), Border Gateway Protocol (BGP), Intermediate System to Intermediate System (IS-IS) to determine the best possible path for data delivery.

Data Link Layer

Data link layer receives and accepts data packet that were being sent by the network layer. Data packets contain IP addresses of sender and receiver. There are two kinds of addressing; logical addressing and physical addressing. Logical addressing is done at network layer where sender and receivers IP addresses are assigned to each segment to form a data packet. Physical addressing is done at data link layer where MAC addresses of sender and receiver are assigned to each data packet to form a frame. MAC addresses are a 12-digit alphanumeric code embedded in network interface card of your computer by your computer manufacturer. The data unit located inside the data link layer is labeled as the "frame". Data link layer is embedded as software in network interface card of the computer and provide means to transfer data from one computer to another via local media. Local media includes copper wire, optical fiber or air for radio signals. Please note, air media does not correspond to audio, video, or animation. It refers to the physical links between two or more computers or networks.

Data Link Layer executes dual basic functions, it permits upper layers of OSI model to retrieve and gain access to the media by means of techniques parallel to framing. It manages and restricts how data is planted and received from media using various modes like the media access control and error detection. Consider two distant hosts; a laptop and a desktop communication with each other. As laptop and desktop are connected to different networks, so they will be using network layer protocols - IP for example, to communicate with each other. In this example, desktop is connected to router r1 through an ethernet cable. Router r1 and r2 are connected via satellite link, and laptop is connected to router r2 via wireless link. Now person1 wants to send some data to laptop, based on the medium used to connect desktop and router r1 data link layer adds some data in the head and tail of IP packet and converts it to a frame. Ethernet frame in this case, router r1 receives this ethernet frame pick up and split into an IP packet and then encapsulate it again to a frame so that it can cross satellite link to reach the router r2. Router r2 will again be encapsulate the frame and encapsulate it again to form a wireless data link frame. Laptop receives this wireless data link frame de-encapsulate it and then forwards the IP packet to network layer.

Finally, data arrives at the application layer.
Application layer protocols then make the received data visible on computer screen. So, network layer or higher-level layers are able to transfer data over media with the help of data link layer. Data link layer lends admittance to the media for higher layers of OSI model. Data link layer also set the oversight on how data is arranged and received from the media. The

technique used to get the frame move the switch between on and then off, the media is named Media Access Control, there may be a number of devices connected to a common media. If there is more than one device that is connected to the same media that sends data at the same time, then there may be a possibility of collision of the two messages resulting in a useless message that neither recipient can understand. To avoid these situations, data link layer keeps an eye on when the shared media is free so that device can transmit data for the receiver. This is called carrier sense multiple access, so data link layer with this media access control methods controls data transmission. Tail of each frame contains bits which are used to detect errors in the received frame. Errors occur due to certain limitations of the media used for transmitting data.

Physical Layer

Till now, data from the application layer has in segmented and compartmented by the transport layer which plays toward the packets by network layer and framed by datalink layer which is a sequence of binary zeroes and ones. Physical layer converts these binary sequences into signal and transmitted over local media. It can be an electrical signal in the case of copper cable or LAN cable, light signal in case of optical fiber and radio signal in case of air. Signal generated by a physical layer depends on the type of media used to connect two devices. At the receiver physical layer receives, converts it to bits and pass it to data link layer as a frame. Frame is further de-encapsulated as data moves through higher layers. Finally, data is moved to application layer. Application layer protocols makes the sender's message visible in the application in the receiver's computer screen. In this way, OSI model is helping to transfer data between distant hosts. These multi-level layers of the OSI model are lying behind the smooth functioning of internet.

Chapter 8: Transmission Control Protocol and Internet Protocol (TCP /IP)

Internet protocols are needed for proper functioning of internet and it includes TCP, HTTP, UDP, FTP, protocols that interact with web browsers while, ARP, ICMP interact with network adapters (IC). Network Protocols are required for Wi-Fi, Bluetooth and LTE to fully function. Network routing protocols are needed for the best download path for a device to download a file or data from the internet. These includes EIGRP, OSPF, and BGP.

TCP/IP

It is a collection of several protocols, but the core functionality of TCP / IP comes from two separate protocols working together, the so-called Transmission Control Protocol (TCP) and Internet Protocol (IP). The job of the TCP is to break up the data from the sending computer into small packets and get these packets ready for transmission. Each packet is given a sequence number at this stage. The content of each packet is used to calculate extra information which is then added to the packet as it's been created the calculation is done again at the receiving end to check for corruption during transmission.

Transmission Control Protocol (TCP)

TCP on the receiving computer reassembles the packets in the correct order according to their sequence numbers and if there are any packets that have been damaged on the way or haven't been received at all, TCP will request that those packets be sent again. You can see them that transmission control protocol is all about ensuring the integrity of the data.

- Breaks data into packets before sending
- Adds error checking information to packets
- Reassembles packets when received
- Requests retransmission of failed packets

Internet Protocol (IP)

The Internet Protocol on the other hand will add addressing information to each packet information to each packet information to identify the intended recipient of the packets. This is the recipient's so-called IP address. The sender's IP address is also added to the packet. The IP addresses also indicate where the recipient and the sender are located. This information is used by the network routers to guarantees that the packets are being dispatched to the right direction.

- Identifies devices on the network
- Routes packets from source to destination via routers

Notes on IP Address:

- Each computer running TCP/IP must have a unique IP address

- 32-bit number expressed as 4 denary octets for convenient notation

- Computers can be statically or dynamically configured (DHCP)

- Subnet mask identifies computer's location on a segmented network

- Default gateway's IP address provides access to the wider network

TCP/ IP Suite of Network Protocols

Other protocols that collectively provide the data transport services utilized by just about everything on the internet

- HyperText Transfer Protocol (HTTP) - This is used over the world wide web, to deliver multimedia rich webpages to your browser.

- File Transfer Protocol (FTP) - Can be used when you want to relocate files quickly between computers

- Simple Mail Transfer Protocol (SMTP) - Used when email messages are sent between mail servers

- Post Office Protocol (POP) - This comes into play when you retrieve email messages from a mail server so you can work with it locally on a PC-based application such as Outlook

- Internet Message Access Protocol (IMAP) - Allows you to work with mail live on the server using webmail system such as Hotmail or Gmail

- Voice Over Internet Protocol (VOIP) - This is specifically for transferring voice and video data over the internet allowing for telephone-style conversations. VOIP is itself a suite of programs.

- User Datagram Protocol (UDP) - A lightweight substitute to TCP. It is much less reliable than TCP because it does not perform any of the error checking, but it is much faster. UDP is suitable for applications where the quality of transmission is not a big issue such as live video stream and online games

- Internet Control Message Protocol (ICMP) – Utilized by routers to exchange status information and error messages. For example, to report that a particular route that cannot be reached

- Address Resolution Protocol (ARP) - allows one device to discover another's MAC address if its IP address is known. Once the target network segment has been reached, the MAC address comes into play

Most TCP/IP packets begin and end their journey on a LAN using ethernet, but IP addresses can only get packets so far, the last leg of the journey depends on each packet bearing the destination MAC address.

How do these protocols work together to get data ready for network transmission?

For our example, let's start with a data we want to transmit, it might be a web page being delivered by a web server to a user's browser. A file being copied from one machine to another.

To begin with, the data must be collected from the application software and formatted for further processing the protocols that performs this task includes - HTTP, FTP, SMTP, and POP3, dependent upon the quality of the data.

Then the data is fragmented down onto packets a sequence number and error-checking data is added to each packet. In addition, something called a "port number" is added to indicate the nature of the data and therefore the application it is heading for. This port number, in concept is different from a physical port on a device that you plug a cable into. Port 80 means that it is HTTP data which is a web page, port 20 is delegated for FTP, while port 25 is SMTP data, and the list goes on. Port numbers are not only used by the receiving application but also by routers to control the movement of certain types of data in a process known as Port Forwarding. Packetizing the data is the job of the TCP.

The source and destination IP addresses are added to each packet, this is essential information for the routers. IP addressing information is added by the Internet Protocol (IP) or ICMP if it is control information.

Finally, the source and destination MAC addresses are added to each packet. MAC addresses are essential for ethernet communication on a LAN segment. Each IP packet is now enclosed within an ethernet frame. Imagine, as if it is a package inside a package. ARP is an example of a protocol that's important when performing this task.

The four distinct layers of software, each layer with a name according to the job of the software operating at that layer. The Application Layer sits at the top, underneath is the Transport Layer, then the Network Layer, and finally the Link Layer at the bottom. This is the so-called four-layer model. The software at each layer can only communicate with what is directly above directly below. The interfaces between these layers now are the rules for passing data from one program to another are standardized and well-known. This means that software from manufacturers like Sun, Microsoft, Cisco, and the open-source community can write new programs to slot in at any position, confident about the compatibility of the programs.

TCP / IP

Transmission Control Protocol and Internet Protocol. It is a series of multi-step protocols that are meant and utilized for connection and communication across the internet. The standard of communication of this suite can be asserted as a client-server model. TCP/IP model is a layered implementation of that OSI, in this case TCP / IP has 4 layers.

Layers of TCP/IP

- Application Layer
- Transport Layer
- Network Layer
- Data Link Layer

All the activities that were being done in the OSI physical model is being covered by these four layers itself.

TCP/IP is a client-server suite, that means the client is sending a request and a server machine is fulfilling that request. In the TCP/IP model, since it is an implementation of the OSI model, there will be different protocols at each level.

Application Layer

HTTP protocol or FTP protocols are used. HTTP Hypertext Transfer Protocol it is the most commonly used protocol for transferring of text, whereas FTP or File Transfer Protocol is used for transferring files.

Transport Layer

This layer uses TCP or Transmission Control Protocol to establish the session between the client machine and the server machine

Network Layer

This stage utilizes Internet Protocol. At this point, all the machines, all the workstations are the nodes even the servers are attached to the TCP/IP network is assigned an IP address. Whatever is the source desk or the destination address that is to be reflected in the form of the IP address. When the client is sending a request, it will give its own address and it will give the IP address of the server machine.

Data Link Layer

The last layer in this structure is where it actually transmits the data physically and it goes to the server machine at server end again at the network layer that data is assembled, until it passes through the entire TCP layers at the server end and the data is assembled completely.

Chapter 9: IP Address

Computers on the Internet communicate with each other with underground or underwater cables or wirelessly. If someone wants to download a file from the internet, then that person's computer should have an address so that other computers in the internet can find and locate my computer. In internet terms, that address of computer is called IP address.

Let us understand it with other examples: If someone wants to send you a mail then that person should know and have your home address, similarly, your computer also needs an address in order for the computers in the internet can send you a file that you want to download.

IP address can be described as a string of numbers written in a certain format. IP address is the shortened term for Internet Protocol Address. An array of guidelines and rules that is responsible to make the internet to function in order, this is what the Internet Protocol is about.

There are two types of IP address; IPv4 and Ipv6

IPv4

This type of IP address consists of 4 numbers separated with a dot in between range. Each number can range from 0 to 255 in decimal numbers, but computers do not understand the decimal numbers so these numbers are converted to binary form which is understandable to computer language. In binary, this range can be written a (00000) Since each number N is represented by a group of a binary digit so the whole IPv4 address is represented by a sequence of 32 ones and zeros or simply by a sequence of 32 bit.

IPv4 is a 32-bit address.

In IPv4 a unique sequence of ones and zeros is assigned to each computer therefore a total of 2 raised to the power of 32 devices, that is approximately 4 billion devices (4,294,967,296 devices) can be addressed and connected to the internet with IPv4.

IPv6

To address the ever-growing number of devices that need to connect to the internet and requires its own IP address, we are slowly moving towards IPv6 which is a 128-bit IP address.

IPv6 is written as a group of 8 hexadecimal numbers separated by colons.

A total of 2 to the power of 128 devices can be connected to the internet   or

340282366920938463463374607431768211456 devices which is far more than enough for many future generations to come.

How to find my IP address?

- To find your computer's public IP address, write "what is my IP" in Google search bar and Google will provide you the information.

- For your smartphone, you can type "what is my IP" in Google search bar or say the command for voice activated search. Again, Google will provide you with the information about your device's public IP address.

Without this protocol, we would not be able to connect to the internet, connect our apps, send messages or calls via the internet and other simple tasks that we tend to overlook, not knowing we need internet for.

Classifications of IP addresses
Dynamic IP Address

When a device like a smartphone or computer is connected to the internet, the Internet Service Provider (ISP) lends the user an IP address from the range of available IP addresses. Once connected, the device now has an IP address in order to browse the internet and to send and receive data to and from the computers in the internet. The next session you connect to the internet, the ISP then provides you with a different IP address within the same available range in their system. Since

IP address keeps on changing every time a device connects to the internet, such IP addresses are called Dynamic IP addresses.

Static IP Address

These are IP addresses that never change. They serve as permanent internet address. It is mostly used by DNS servers (these are servers that help us to open a website on our end). Static IP addresses provides information such as which device is located in which continent, which country, which city and which ISP is providing the internet connection to the device. Once the ISP is known, trace location of the device can be done in no time. Static IP address are considered somewhat less secure than Dynamic IP address because they are easier to track. However, following safe internet practices can help you to keep your computer secure.

Dynamic Host Configuration Protocol (DHCP)

Each digital device that resides within a network is required to have an IP
 address for communication purposes. An IP address is an identifier for a computer or device on a network. There are two ways that a computer can be assigned an IP address, it could be done by using a Static IP or Dynamic IP.
Static IP is where a user assigns a computer or device with an IP address manually. This was the original method that was

done in the beginning of networking. Each digital device that resides within a network, the user would want to obtain computer's network configuration page and manually type in an IP address. In addition to an IP address, it was also required to type in other information such as the Subnet Mask, then the Default Gateway, and lastly a DNS Server. In cases when there is another computer or device needed to be added to the network, the process needs to be repeated again. This process was tedious and requires a lot of work especially if the user is dealing with a large network that has a lot of computers. It was also important to remember that each computer has a unique IP addresses assigned, because if the same IP address is used twice in the same network it would cause an IP conflict. Those computers with conflicting IP addresses will not have the ability to gain access to the network.

A better and easier way of assigning computers an IP address was made - the Dynamic IP.

The set up where a DHCP server voluntary provides an IP address to a computer is called Dynamic IP. A DHCP server automatically assigns a computer an IP address, it can also assign a subnet mask, a default gateway, and a DNS server.

As an example, at the Network Connection Properties window for the Network Interface Card (NIC) on a Microsoft Windows computer. In there, an option to set 'Obtain an IP address automatically' is available. When this option is selected, the computer would broadcast a request for an IP address on the network then the DHCP server will assign an IP address from its pool and deliver it to the computer. Once it is done, the user can verify all the different settings that the DHCP server has given the computer and the user can do this by opening up a Command Prompt and then type in the keyword "ipconfig" space forward slash all [ipconfig /al] then press enter. It should show that DHCP is enabled on the computer, which means it is getting its IP address from a DHCP server. Other information that will be displayed: the DNS server, default gateway, subnet mask and most importantly the IP address - all configurations were provided by DHCP server. The Dynamic IP Addressing is the preferred choice by many because it is automatic, and it makes managing a network a lot easier.

The DHCP server assigns IP addresses to computers on a network from its scope. A scope is a spectrum of IP addresses that are being handed out by the DHCP server. These values can be customized to either increasing or decreasing the range, it all depends on what the network administrator prefers.

The servers assign the IP addresses as a lease, so the computer does not actually own the IP address. A lease is the amount of time an IP address is designated to a digital device within the network. For example, a lease of IP could be for one day. The reason behind the concept of lease is to help make sure that

the DHCP does not run out of IP addresses in its scope. After a certain period of time during the lease, the computers will transmit a signal to the DHCP server asking the
server to renew its lease of the IP address. In some ways, the computers in the network are informing the DHCP server that it is still present on the system and its IP address is still being used. If a computer is removed from the network, that device is not going to be able to ask the DHCP server for a renewal, and if it does not ask a renewal then the lease will expire. The IP address from the computer with expired lease, will go back to the IP address pool, it is now renewed and can now be used for another computer.

If a network administrator prefers for a computer within a network to have a specific IP address all the time meaning the IP address would not change, one option is to create a reservation on the DHCP server. A reservation ensures that a specific computer that has been recognized by its MAC address will always be given the same IP address when that computer or device seeks the DHCP server for an IP address. Reservations are not typically given to regular computers, it is typically allocated to special devices or computers such as network printers, servers, routers, or something similar; because devices like these should be given the same IP address constantly.

Notes:

- DHCP is a service that runs on a server such as Microsoft server or a Linux server.
- It is also a service that runs on routers, whether it is a business router or a small office/ home office router, these routers will have a DHCP service built into them.

Chapter 10: Domain Name System (DNS)

DNS

Across the internet, computers can distinguish a device's identity with a distinctive and one of a kind identifier called the IP address. Computers cannot comprehend nor understand human vocabulary. If computers cannot comprehend and understand the human vocabulary, then if you are wondering how can a computer pull up a webpage whenever we put in a site's URL on the address bar? The simplest answer to that inquiry: DNS

For example, a person who only knows how to speak English would want to communicate with another person, but that person only knows Mandarin. To have a successful communication, a translator would be vital. The concept is similar when it comes to the internet. The digital side of the conversation, the computers, can discern IP addresses. Its counterpart in this conversation, humans, can only comprehend our own language. The DNS operates as a decoder that is placed in the middle of the two participants of the conversation.

The DNS controls and manages a table where names or identifiers have been charted into numbers, especially the domain names of websites that are charted to its corresponding IP addresses. When a user keys in google.com in the address bar, the DNS converts it to the language that the web browser can comprehend which in this case would be the IP address and hands it off to the web browser. The web browser recognized the command that the user needs to reach Google's website, it makes an attempt to reach the Google server and loads its website on the computer. The DNS functions like a phone book of the internet whenever computer seeks with identifiers to obtain numbers.

How DNS works internally?

To understand this, we should know what our DNS servers.

Servers are computers storing HTML files, images, sounds, videos, or any other file types. Servers that work together to provide IP address of the requested website to the web browser are called DNS Servers.

Types of DNS Servers:

- DNS recursive resolver / DNS resolver
- Root name server
- Top Level Domain / TLD name server
- Authoritative name server

DNS resolver is furnished by the ISP. It conjoins the web browser of our digital devices, like the computer, to the DNS name servers. The series of root name servers are currently counted to be at thirteen at the moment. It is rationally called letter.root-servers.net ; it is regulated and managed by twelve various organizations. The spectrum of letters, with the only exception of the letter g, are from letters a up to m. For every particular series, a number of servers are situated throughout the globe. The informational page is present for all root name servers at letter.root-servers.org ; the information is organized alphabetically with an exception of the letter g. The letter g is the home page. For the domains that are using a common domain extension, the TLD name server keeps all of its information. To illustrate this, .com TLD name server manages and preserves the data and materials of all websites with the .com extension; .net TLD name server manages and preserves the data and materials of all websites with the .net extension. In the domain name system, the authoritative name server is conclusive stop in the chain. It safe keep the IP address of the website that is being asked for. By using certain CMD commands, the authoritative name server for a website can be detected.

(nslookup, set query=ns, etc)

What is master and the slave DNS?

The slave is the absolute likeness of master DNS and is utilized to distribute the DNS server load

How a computer loads a website?

If a user types in facebook.com in the address bar of a web browser, since the internet needs an IP address, so it transmits the inquiry to the operating system of the computer. The OS is engineered to transmit the inquiry to the DNS resolver. The OS then establishes a communication with the DNS resolver. The DNS resolver monitors its cache if the IP address of the website that is being requested is present. If not, the root name server receives the inquiry from the DNS. The root name server examines the website's extension to find out if it is a .com or .org or .net . Knowing what the extension is at this point, the IP address of the TLD name server can now be provided by the root name server to the DNS resolver.

For this sample context, the DNS resolver provides the IP address of the .com TLD name server, the DNS resolver contacts the .com TLD name server, it lends the IP address of the authoritative name server that shall automatically save the information which is the IP address of the sought website. Lastly, the authoritative name server allocates the correct IP address of facebook.com to the DNS resolver. This information is kept and saved by the DNS resolver in its cache, this information is ready to be used whenever it is needed again. The operating system of the computer also receives a copy of the IP address so it can store its information. The web browser then receives the information that was forwarded to it by the operating system. The web browser then reaches out to the

Facebook server and displays facebook.com - the website that was originally requested by the user.

How TLD name server knows which authoritative name server stores the IP address of the requested website?

It starts when a domain name is bought and acquired from a registrar. There are several providers in the market today, for this scenario let us use WordPress. The domain that shall utilize as the authoritative name server can be designated on the registrar's website. From the time that a web hosting plan is acquired, for example - Amazon Web Hosting, the specifics of the authoritative name server can be obtained. As soon as the registrar's website receives the specifics of the authoritative nameserver, the TLD name servers managing the authority registry get a directive from the registrar to amend TLD name server with the particulars of the authoritative name server that the user has supplied. The precise IP address of the requester website can be generated since the TLD name server has identified which authoritative nameserver can accomplish it.

Is DNS important?

As a part of product research conducted by a Europe-based internet provider in 2016, they methodically surveyed 2,000 people and were surprised to learn that only 1 in 5 people can easily recall their home phone number or have memorized in some way. In a study done in 2019 by a medical diagnostic company based in the United States, only 57% of 1004 adult respondents know confidently what their blood type is.

Phone numbers and blood type are important information that we cannot easily remember, and that's ok. But imagine for every website you need to visit, whether it is Google, Facebook, Twitter or Netflix, you have to remember a set of numbers just to get on their webpage. It could be so daunting for a lot of us!

Domain Name System or more commonly referred to as DNS Servers is a computer server that houses the data on public IP addresses and its corresponding hostname.

Chapter 11: Remote Access Protocols, Network Storage Systems & File Transfer Protocols

Remote Access Protocols

- ### Remote Access Service (RAS)

This is a technology that enables the user to connect to a computer from a remote location. For example; accessing an office computer while the user is miles away at home. It allows the services on a remote network to be accessed over a dial-up connection. This service was originally engineered by Microsoft and built into the older Windows operating system (NT line of server software). It works with most of the major set of protocols suchlike as NetBeui, IPX / SPX, and TCP / IP

- ### Serial Line Internet Protocol (SLIP)

This is a protocol that is designed for communication between two computers using serial connection, such as a typical phone line. SLIP is rarely used anymore because it is not a secure protocol. During a dial - up connection, it sends all the data including sensitive data like passwords in clear text. This protocol falls short in today's need for security when it comes to data - handling. SLIP does not provide any error - checking and is limited to only utilizing the TCP / IP protocol - a better protocol was needed to address these issues.

- **Point - To - Point Protocol (PPP)**

This was the answer to the SLIP's pressing issues. This is a standard remote access protocol that is being used even to this day. It was developed to replace SLIP's limitation in security, error - checking and protocol support. Like SLIP that is used for communication between two computers using a serial connection such a typical phone line. Unlike SLIP, PPP is a secure protocol, it supports encryption and authentication. Most internet service providers (ISP) utilize this protocol for their customers who may opt to access the internet through a dial up connection.

- **Point - To - Point Protocol Over Ethernet (PPPoE)**

The moniker is exactly what it implies. This protocol uses PPP over Ethernet (Note: refer to the text for PPP for its details). The PPPoE works by encapsulating PPP in ethernet frames. The users of this protocol are typically connected to the internet via DSL broadband, cable modem, or wireless connection. It was also developed for connecting multiple users within a local area network towards a remote site sharing a common device.

- **Point - To - Point Tunneling Protocol (PPTP)**

This technology is utilized for establishing Virtual Private Networks (VPN). In fact, this is the default protocol associated with VPNs. PPTP ensures that the data transfer from one device to another is secure by creating a secure tunnel between the two points.

- **Generic Route Encapsulation (GRE)**

This is a protocol that is used along with Point - To - Point Tunneling Protocol (PPTP) as part of creating a VPN network. GRE is what actually creates the tunnel in PPTP. It is used to encapsulate the data in a highly secure method.

- **Virtual Private Network (VPN)**

This is a secluded or a private network that utilizes a public network, such as the internet, in order to establish or create a remote connection. The data is encrypted as it sends and decrypted as received. It provides a dedicated link between two points over the internet.

Network Storage Systems

Network Attached Storage (NAS)

This storage system is ideal if the user / network administrator wanted to set up a network storage in a way that stored data goes to a centralized location where it can be accessed from all of the devices that are connected on the network. This can be done by using a network attached device. A NAS is designed for storing data and it does not do anything else besides storing data. Typically, a NAS is a box that will have multiple hard drives in a RAID configuration for redundancy. It will also have a network interface card (NIC) that will directly attach to a switch or router in order for the data to be accessed over a network. Once it is on and active within the network, it can be accessed from other devices such as desktops, laptops, servers, and it can be accessed as a shared drive.

NAS can be ideally used in homes and are more typically present in home office or small to medium-sized businesses. A main disadvantage of utilizing the NAS is how it has a sole point of failure, to put in more context – if a component fails power supply on the NAS then all of the other devices will not have the ability to access its data.

Storage Area Network (SAN)

This storage system is engineered as a special high-speed network device that stores and provides access to large amounts of data. Ideally, it is a dedicated network that is used for data storage. This network consists of multiple disk arrays, switches, and servers. Since it is composed of multiple components, a SAN is fault tolerant while still having the data being shared among several disk arrays. In the event that a switch, or a disk array, or if a server goes down or have a malfunction, the data can still be accessed. Whenever a server accesses the data on a SAN, it accesses the data as if it was a local hard drive because that is how operating systems (OS) recognize a SAN. It is recognized as a local attached hard drive rather than a shared network drive like in a NAS. Another advantage of using NAS is how highly scalable it can be, adding more storage space can easily be done without interruption on the network.

SAN is a high-speed network and that is because in a SAN, all the devices are interconnected - all of the devices are connected to each other and it uses fiber channel to link with each other. Fiber channel is a standard for SAN, because it is fiber optics it has the speed capability of between gigabits per second all the way up to 128 gigabits per second making it extremely fast hence, making it expensive. As an alternative to fiber channel, some SANs have also been using iSCSI (Internet Small Computer System Interface) instead which is a more affordable alternative but not as fast as the fiber channel.

Another important factor about SAN is how it is not affected by network traffic such as bottleneck that can occur in a local area network (LAN), this is because SANs are configured not to be part of a local area network. SANs are partitioned off; it is basically a network all by itself.

Due to the design and trade off price of SANs, it is mainly used by large companies and large organizations.

Standard Protocols

Hypertext Transfer Protocol (HTTP)

Hypertext Transfer Protocol or HTTP; this is possibly the most widely used protocol in the world today. HTTP is the protocol that is used for viewing web pages on the internet. So, when you type in a web address like google.com, you'll notice that HTTP is automatically at the beginning of the web address after you hit enter, this indicates that you are now using HTTP to retrieve this web page. Now in standard HTTP, all the information is sent in clear text, so all the information that is exchanged between your computer and that web server which includes any text that you type on that website that information is transferred over the public internet and because it is transferred in clear text, it is vulnerable to anybody who wants it such as hackers. Now normally this would not be a big deal if you were just browsing regular websites and no sensitive data such as passwords or credit card information are being used but if you were to type in personal sensitive data like your name, address, phone number, date of birth, password or SSN, that sensitive data goes from your computer and then it has to travel across the public internet to get to that web server and this makes your data vulnerable because a hacker that somewhere on the internet listen in as the data is being transferred and steal your information. "So, a hacker can steal personal information as it is traveling over the internet, he has a name, phone number, address, credit card number and other information. "This is a problem as far as security and this why HTTP was developed.

Hypertext Transfer Protocol Secure (HTTPS)

Stands for Secure Hypertext Transfer Protocol. This is HTTP with a security feature. Secure HTTP encrypts that is being retrieved by HTTP, it ensures that all the data that is being moved and relocated across the internet among computers and servers is secure by making the data impossible to read and it does this by using encryption algorithms to scramble the data that is being transferred. For example, if you were to go to a website that requires you to enter personal information such as passwords or credit card information, you will notice that an S will be added to the HTTP in the web address and this S indicates that you are now using secure HTTP and have entered a secure where sensitive data is going to be passed and that data is going to be protected. In addition to the S being added, a lot of web browsers will also show a padlock symbol in the address bar to indicate that secure HTTP is being used. So, by using secure HTTP, all the data which includes anything that you type is no longer sent in clear text, it is scrambled in an unreadable form as it travels across the internet. So, if a hacker tries to steal your information, he would get a bunch of meaningless data because the data is encrypted, and the hacker would not be able to crack the encryption to unscramble the data.

SSL

Secure Socket Layer

Secure HTTP protects the data by using one of two protocols. One of these protocols is the Secure Socket Layer or SSL. It is a set of rules that is used to ensure security on the internet. It uses public key encryption to secure data. This is how SSL works: when a computer connects to a website that is using SSL, the computer's web browser will ask the website to identify itself then the web server will send the computer a copy of its SSL certificate.

An SSL certificate is a small digital certificate that is used to authenticate the identity of a website. Basically, it is used to let your computer know that the website you're visiting is trustworthy. Your computer's browser will check to make sure that it trusts the certificate and if it does it will send a communication to the web server then after the web server will respond back with an acknowledgement so when SSL session can proceed, then after all these steps are complete, encrypted data can now be exchanged between your computer and the web server.

TLS

Transport Layer Protocol is the other protocol being used by secure HTTP. TLS is the latest industry standard cryptographic protocol. It is the successor to SSL, and it is based on the same specifications and like SSL, it also authenticates the server, client, and encrypts the data. It is also important to point out that a lot of websites are now using secure HTTP by default regardless is sensitive data is going to be exchanged or not. A lot of this has to do with Google, because they are now flagging websites as not secure if they are not protected with SSL and if a website is not SSL-protected, Google will penalize that website in their search rankings. This is one of the major reasons, you'll notice that secure HTTP is being used rather than standard HTTP.

File Transfer Protocols

Protocols that are used to transfer files over network.

File Transfer Protocol (FTP)

FTP is a standard set of rules that is used to move or relocate files among computers and servers above a network, the internet is a good example of it. In a nutshell, FTP is the language that computers use to transfer files over a TCP / IP network.

A sample scenario of using the FTP: When a computer user somewhere in the world wanted to make their files available for other people to download, all that user needs to do is to simply have the file that is meant to be shared, uploaded to the FTP and then other people from anywhere in the world can simply connect to that FTP server and download the files using the FTP protocol. A dedicated FTP server can be used but is not always necessary to do this type of file transfer, a simple workstation or computer can be configured to act as an FTP server. In Microsoft Windows, this can be done using the Internet Information Services Manager.

There are a couple of ways to transfer files using the FTP

- Internet Browser
- FTP Client
- Command Prompt

For example, a user wants to download a few mp3 files that someone else has put on the FTP server. One way of retrieving the files is by using an internet browser. On the browser's address bar, type in the address of the FTP server that is intended to be reached, as if just going to a regular website. In other words, type in the FTP address as the URL.

The only difference between going to a regular website and accessing an FTP server via web browser is the prefix that needs to be used. In web browsing "HTTP" or "HTTPS" are the prefix that can be used, in FTP it is simply "FTP" as the prefix to be used.

Once the user has reached the FTP server site, folders and files can easily be browsed depending on what the owner has made available. The user can simply view and download the file.

In most cases, FTP servers will require an account with a username and password. Though there are some FTP servers that lets users to login anonymously. It just depends on the type of authentication the owner of the FTP server has set up.

Another way to connect to an FTP server is by using an FTP client. There are a number of FTP clients available for use, an example of a commonly - used and free FTP client is Filezilla. Using an FTP client provides a graphical user interface which can attribute to a better overall experience than using a web browser. Once connected to an FTP server using an FTP client, users can drag and drop the files that it wants to be downloaded. For some users who have permission access, it is easier to upload files to the FTP server using the FTP client.

Today, accessing FTP server via the Windows command prompt is mostly used whenever there is a software repair needs to be done in the system. This happens mostly whenever the web browser and FTP client are either not available or not working. This can be caused by malware, virus or corrupted files.

Transferring files is a common use of FTP especially for transferring files in bulk. Another common use of FTP is to give the ability web designers to upload files to their web servers.

A drawback of using the FTP is how it is not a secure protocol. The data that is being transferred is not encrypted. All the data that is being moved is sent in clear text which can cause security concerns. Ideally, FTP should only be used on a limited basis or on trust - worthy networks or better yet when the data that is being transferred is not sensitive because of its minimal level of security protocol.

Secure File Transfer Protocol (SFTP)

If a user needs to transfer data that needs to be protected, then a more secure transfer protocol should be used. Here is where SFTP becomes practical. Secure FTP is just like its predecessor, the FTP, except it adds a layer of security. The data using Secure FTP is fully encrypted by utilizing secure shell during data transfer. In this way, no data is being sent in clear text, it is all encrypted. Secure FTP authenticates both the user and the server, and it uses port 22.

It is also important to note that both FTP and SFTP are connection - oriented protocols that use Transmission Control Protocol (TCP) for file transfer, so it guarantees file delivery.

Trivial File Transfer Protocol (TFTP)

This is an absolute straightforward protocol for file transferring; however, it is not meant to send files over the internet unlike with FTP and SFTP does. It is used mainly for transferring files within a local area network (LAN). It is often used to transfer configuration files and firmware images to network devices such as firewalls and routers. TFTP is more often used by network admins rather than for home users. Unlike FTP and SFTP that uses TCP protocol to transfer files, TFTP is a connectionless protocol that uses the User Datagram Protocol (UDP) instead. Since the TFTP is utilizing UDP instead of TCP, it is unreliable protocol. Lastly, TFTP does not provide any security and not does it need to since it is used for local area network and not over the internet.

Chapter 12: SECURITY PROTOCOLS

Defense in Depth Principle

There are threats to every system and several ways an attacker may try to exploit them. When we consider how to secure a system, we need to consider Defense in Depth.

The *Defense in Depth Principle* states that there is no one thing or even two that can completely secure a system. This contention is that if one part of the security solution would have failed then another part should be able to resist or prevent the attack from succeeding.

In practice, this means applying security in layers. For example: we could have a firewall and an IPS (Intrusion Prevention System) on the edge of the network, behind the firewall there may be an email scanning service, and on the workstations, there would be antivirus software.

An attacker may try to send some malicious code through email, the firewall and IPS may not be able to pick this up as email is a valid application. In this scenario, we would rely on the email scanner.

But what if the email scanner service is down for whatever reason? Maybe it crashed or maybe it just did not pick up that this email is a threat. In that case, we still have the antivirus software on the workstation to fall back on.

This example is a simplified look at the Defense in Depth. This strategy reduces the risk of a successful and possibly very expensive security breach.

A common misconception in network security for beginners is to rely too heavily on the firewall. All too often people think that the firewall should suffice. Unfortunately, that is just not true. Firewalls are only just a piece of a much larger puzzle. A simple firewall uses IP address and ports to allow or deny traffic. An IPS can look into this information further and deeply into the traffic to see if it matches known patterns of attacks. These two are just part of the edge of the network.

What about encrypting traffic with HTTPS, requiring authentication and authorization before accessing secure resources. New security flaws are found regularly, patching these flaws regularly would definitely help with the security of the network systems. Also, we need to consider our endpoints - workstations, laptops, smartphones, and any other device that connects to the network. This is where we think about antivirus, host-based firewalls, and VPN (Virtual Private Network) connections.

We cannot consider something to be reasonably secured without considering all aspects of the systems. Aside from the technical controls like firewalls and antivirus, but there are also other things to consider like the physical and administrative controls. We need to consider things like the security of the building where the servers or workstations are based, locking the door to the server room, or putting equipment in locked racks or cabinets. When it comes to administrative controls, these relate to policies and procedures. It can start with identifying the proper way to handle data, a big part of this is simply educating the users. Having controlled set of who can access the data. Reminding the users to use strong passwords, how to avoid social engineering, and how to recognize threats in general.

Security should be applied in layers and these layers are more than just technical controls. Having a contingency plan in the event one of the security layers failed, what actions can be taken to put everything back together and minimize the threat or damage.

Intrusion Prevention Service (IPS)

Intrusion Prevention Service is designed to prevent malicious actions from occurring within the network. For modern implementations, we always deal with IPS than IDS (Intrusion Detection System) since aside from preventing malicious actions, it also logs each incident where malicious actions have been prevented.

IPS can be either network based (NIPS) or host based (HIPS). The network-based monitors the entire network for malicious traffic by analyzing all tcp/ip traffic entering the network. The host based on the other hand, monitors a single host for malicious activity, usually for unauthorized changes.

NIPS requires that IPS be installed on a device at the network perimeter. The HIPS require that IPS be installed on every host that requires protections - usually it is only installed on specific servers.

IPS detection can be signature-based or anomaly-based. There is always one signature for every exploit that is capable of preventing, the signature works by zeroing in on some unique aspect of the particular exploit that is always present. One of the advantages of this method is the low rate of false-positives. On the other hand, signature based can only detect exploits for which a signature exists, so signatures must always be updated.

In anomaly-based, the system looks for abnormal traffic and assumes that the abnormal traffic is malicious. The advantage of this method - it requires less maintenance; it does not need to be updated constantly. The only downside with the anomaly-based is the higher rate of false-positives.

Newer IPS systems are primarily signature-based employed in a physical security device. This is highly recommended for the needs of the majority of networks. Signature-based IPS can be put on a physical security client such as a firewall that sits on the perimeter of the network. A subscription is typically needed to be obtained from the vendor to keep the signatures up to date. Generally, the signatures updates automatically, on a daily basis similar to how antivirus does its updates.

Types of threat:
- DoS (denial of service)
- Ransomware
- Phishing
- Data theft
- Tracking
- Botnet

Sources of Threats

Threat actors: Individuals with malicious intent, nation state sponsored groups

Sources of Vulnerabilities

Design problems

When somebody has designed an application or a system and there's just a fundamental problem with that design

Implementation flaws

The design is fine but actually when that design has been translated into the appropriate code, will probably be at hardware, there's problem at that stage and there's resulting in weaknesses

Configuration issues

This is quite common. Systems are insecure when it shouldn't be, because somebody either misunderstood how to configure the item

Changes over time

Too many changes have been done to the point that the system is no longer secure because the original intent has been lost

Failure to provide security updates

Most of the recent security attacks have been successful purely because people have not applied security updates.

Assumption of trust

Devices that do not belong to the network are plugged to the computer, making it the network system highly vulnerable for phishing scams. Email attachments that we easily open without examining a few details.

Vulnerabilities: Wi-Fi

- Do you control the hardware?
- Do you control the software / firmware?
- Are the protocols broken?
- Who have you given access to? Are their systems secure?
- Whose network have you connected to?
- Non-physical connection increases attack surface

Risk Management

- Apply security in layers
- Know your gear
- Port scanning - a sample program is Nmap
- Firewall logging
- Intrusion Detection and Intrusion Prevention Service

Risk Management: Wi-Fi

- SSID hiding doesn't work
- WEP is broken
- Don't use SSIDs that can make you a target

Wireless Security

Most of us had connected to a Wi-Fi network with our laptop, tablet, or our smartphones. To join a network connection with a device, a network name needs to be selected and a password needs to be supplied.

Wi-Fi network can be just open with no password required; in that scenario it means anybody can join it. However, in the majority of cases, Wi-Fi networks will be secure and will require a password. There are several different protocols for securing a Wi-Fi network.

Wired Equivalent Privacy (WEP)

This protocol was developed in 1999 making it the earliest security protocol that was used for wireless networks. As the term suggests, it is meant to supply an equal level of security to wireless networks as it did for wired networks. However, this turned out not to be 100 percent the case, it was learned that the 40-bit encryption that WEP used was vulnerable and not secure making it easily hackable. This is the main reason why WEP is no longer used today and modern Wi-Fi routers won't even have it as an option anymore.

Wi-Fi Protected Access (WPA)

After WEP, better security protocol was needed for wireless networks. WPA is a wireless security protocol that was developed to solve the problems of WEP. WPA uses a stronger encryption method called Temporary Key Integrity Protocol (TKIP). The new encryption method dynamically changes its keys as it is being used that way it ensures the data integrity. Even though WPA is a lot more secure than WEP, even today the WPA is outdated. TKIP did eventually have some vulnerabilities.

WPA2

WPA2 was developed to provide even stronger security than WPA, it does this by requiring the use of a stronger encryption method. While WPA uses TKIP for encryption, WPA2 uses AES which stands for Advanced Encryption Standard. The newer encryption uses a symmetric encryption algorithm which makes it strong enough to resist a brute-force attack. In fact, AES is classified to be secure that the U.S. federal government has adopted to use it, it is being utilized to encrypt sensitive government data.

Now when you log in to the Wi-Fi router's configuration page and proceed to the Wi-Fi security section, this is where you would find the different security protocols that you can choose from to protect your Wi-Fi network. In most routers, there is an option that has both WPA and WPA2 - this is a mixed security option. This option enables WPA and WPA2 at the same time, it will use both TKIP and AES security. The reason for this option is for compatibility purposes because some older devices (dated prior to 2006) may not be compatible with using AES encryption that is being used with WPA2. In this option, older devices will connect to the older WPA protocol, but at the same time modern devices will connect to WPA2.

Using the mixed option all the time, though it is the most compatible with all devices, with this option while it uses AES it also is utilizing TKIP which is the lesser secure encryption. This leaves your network more vulnerable to a breach.

WPA3

This is the next generation of wireless security; it was introduced in 2018. According to the Wi-Fi Alliance, WPA3 contributes top of the line security protocols available for commerce. To facilitate further vigorous authentication, additional features were placed to streamline Wi-Fi security. It will also receive increased protection from password guessing attempts. The WPA3 option is available to newer routers.

Wi-Fi Protected Setup (WPS)

This is another type of wireless security method that does not require the user to type in a password. The WPS was designed for people who know a little or novice about wireless networks, to make it easy as possible for their devices to join a wireless network.

There are a couple of different methods that are used with WPS, but by far the most common method is the Push Button method. In this method the user would just need to press a couple of buttons to be connected to the network.

Most routers today will have a physical WPS button that you can press, and a lot of Wi-Fi printers will also have a software or physical WPS button.

For example, you want to connect a printer via WPS, you would need to push and hold the WPS button that is located on the Wi-Fi router and in the span of 120 seconds you would press the WPS button on your printer. After a few seconds, the printer should be connected to the Wi-Fi router.

Another method for WPS is if the client you are using has a WPS pin number. If this is the set-up, the user just needs to enter a pin number to the field provided and within a few seconds it will connect to the network.

WPS is the easiest way to join a wireless network, a lot of manufacturers have built wireless products with WPS. This is just to make it as simple as possible for the users to join a device to a wireless network.

ACCESS CONTROL

Access Control is called MAC filter in some routers, with this option the network administrator can either allow or block devices from joining a network. Every network adapter has a MAC address (MAC address can be described as the hexadecimal number - numeral system made up of 16 symbols, that exclusively pinpoint the identity of each device that resides on a network) and with Access Control the network administrator can manage the devices that can and cannot connect to the network using the MAC address of the specific device. When a device is blocked, it would exclusively be able to obtain an IP address from the router, but it would not be able to communicate with any other device and it would not be able to connect to the internet.

The Access Control can be used as an extra layer of security that is in addition to the network's Wi-Fi password. Access Control also works for wired devices.

Chapter 13: BASIC NETWORK UTILITIES

PING Utility

The ping command is the most widely used of all network utilities. It is a tool that is used to test issues such as network connectivity and name resolution

In a sample scenario given, if a user would ping a host IP address: At a command prompt, then the user needs to type "ping" space, then the IP address of the host then hit enter. The command will send out four data packets to the destination IP address we chose, then the destination will send back those packets to you as a reply. These replies are called Echo Reply Requests. These replies will tell you what is happening to the destination host you tried to ping. For instance, 4 packets sent, and 4 packets received, and 0 loss means there is a general connectivity between you and the destination. If you did not get a reply, that means there is no reply from the host, and it could mean there is no network connectivity between you and the destination.

In some cases, you might get a result from a ping that says, "request timed out", this could mean that the host network is down, or it is blocking all the ping requests.

Another message that you might get is "destination host unreachable", that message is coming from the router, that means that the route to the destination cannot be found.

The ping command can also be used to test DNS name resolution issues. Instead of using the IP address in the ping command, try using the domain name of the website you are trying to reach. For example, type "ping" space, the domain name, then hit enter. If by pinging the domain name, if you get the same successful result as typing the IP address when you ping the same destination, then this would indicate that the name resolution by the DNS is working fine.

If you ping the domain name and it failed, then the next step is typing the ip address instead. If by typing the IP address and the ping is successful this time, then you can isolate the issue to DNS

Trace Route Utility

Tracert is used to find the exact path the data packet is taking on its way to the destination.

For example: to trace a route from one computer to another, key in "tracert" space, then the destination computer's IP address at the command prompt,

then press enter. By doing this, the data packet will find its way to the destination. Each time the data reaches a router on its path, it will report back information about that router such as its IP address and the time it took between each hop.

TraceRT utility is a great tool that can be used to pinpoint where the problem lies within a network if the data cannot reach its destination.

IPCONFIG

This is a useful tool to display network configurations for your computer and this information can be used as part of the problem-solving process.

- Ipconfig – shows the default gateway, the IP address, and the subnet mask
- Ipconfig /all – shows the full TCP/IP configuration
- Ipconfig /renew - releases and renew the IP address lease
- Ipconfig /release - releases the IP address lease

Chapter 14: NETWORKING ISSUES

Most network designs can be classified as either wired or wireless. Networks do not have to use either types of networks solely, but it can certainly be combined. If you have a wireless network, there is a possibility that at one point a wired connection existed within your network.

Most businesses today adopt the usage of incorporating both wired and wireless networks due to ease of access and business needs. It is important to know how to diagnose problems related to wired and wireless issues.

Wired Factors

A common fault point is the media. In a wired network, this involves copper cables. Overtime, cables can become worn out or damaged which makes it prone to short circuits. It is also important to remember to use the right type of cable depending on what kind of network you are using.

If you are going to use copper cabling, it is important to recognize the environment around the cable because certain electronic equipment that might seem harmless (like fluorescent lights, microwave ovens, fans, etc.) can interfere with the copper media therefore altering or reducing the strength of the signal which is known as attenuation.

Another factor to consider is the length of the cable. If the cable exceeds the maximum recommended length, then this could also cause problems within the network. Using the wrong type of cable could be another cause of network issue, for example you are using a crossover cable, but your network requires straight cable.

Wireless Factors

Antennas are another factor that affects wireless service. Since wireless devices operate using radio waves, the antenna is a big factor that can determine the range and speed of a signal.

- Omni-directional antenna - one of the most common types of antenna. This type of antenna transmits signal in all directions. Every wireless device within its direction can pick up its signal as long as the device is in range

- Directional antenna - this type directs the signal to one direction. That direction is to wherever the antenna is pointed to.

Problems that can arise in a wireless environment one of these is an interference. Microwave ovens can cause interference and certain wireless devices can interfere with the network's wireless signal (like mobile phones, Bluetooth devices such as a wireless keyboard and mouse). The waves that are being produced by other wireless devices can alter the signal of a wireless network.

A cordless phone is another device that is known to cause issues to wireless networks, that is because a lot of this type of phone operates on the same frequency as wireless routers do. An example of this issue is when the wireless phone rings and it affects the network connectivity of a laptop. This happens if both the wireless network and wireless phone are using the same wireless channel. To quickly resolve this, you can log on to the router's configuration page and change the channel in the wireless signal - this should take care of it most of the time.

The structure of a building is another factor that can affect a wireless signal. Depending on the materials used and structured in the building like concrete walls, window film, and metal studs - these can all have an effect on the strength and stability of the wireless signal. If this scenario occurs, the placing of the router needs to be in a strategic location within the building.

Wrong Encryption

Using the wrong type of encryption could prevent other devices from joining a network. This might happen if a router is using a newer encryption method like WPA2 in its wireless network but a device like a laptop is using an older encryption like WEP or WPA, the laptop would not be able to join the wireless network because the newer encryption may not be recognized by older devices.

Link LED (Light Emitting Diode)

Simple indicators that are used to tell us basic information about a network device. On a network interface card (NIC), if network cable is plugged in to the NIC port then a green led light indicates a successful network connection has been established, this is called the link light. If after connecting the cable and the indicator does not light up, this might indicate an issue such as a bad cable or simply the computer is turned off. A yellow blinking light indicates there is network activity whether the speed of the light's blinking is fast or not, this indicates normal operation.

One of the most obvious things to check when it comes to network connectivity issue is the physical connectivity. Check to see if your computer is connected to the network. Thoroughly examine the led indicators. See if the switch is turned on. Check for loose cables either from the NIC or switch connection.

Troubleshooting Strategy

1. Determine the manifestations of the issues and its likely cause
- Gather information about the problem

- What is the problem?
- When did the problem occur?
- Specific error messages
- Does the problem happen all the time or intermittently?

2. Identify the affected area
- Is the problem isolated or spread across several locations
- If the problem affects everyone, check the switch
- If the problem is isolated, check individual cable

3. Establish what has changed: problem do not occur at random; it happens for a reason.
- Did anything change just prior to the problem happening?
- Was there any hardware removed or added?
- Was there any software installed or uninstalled?
- Was anything downloaded from the internet?

4. Select the most probable cause
- Look for the simplest solutions first
- Does the device have power?
- Are the cables plugged in?
- Check the LEDs

5. Carry out a game plan and resolution as well as its probable effects
- This is the cautious phase
- Must know what effect the action will have on the network
- Will it affect the entire network or be isolated at one area?

6. Test the result
- Where you drive the operation to resolve the obstacle
- Where you will know if the resolution strategy will iron out the obstacle at hand or not

7. Pinpoint the conclusion and the aftermath of the resolution
- Has the solution strategy fix the dilemma or not?
- What effect did it have on everyone else?
- Do the results show a temporary fix or a permanent one?

8. Document the solution and the process
- Document the problem
- Document what caused the problem
- Document how the problem was fixed
- This is an important step. If the problem has been resolved it is important to document what transpired

within the issue and how was it resolved. In the event that the same issue occurs again, you or anyone who has access to that documentation would know the resolution in the fastest possible time and may take preventive measures so the problem will not occur again.

Conclusion

Thank you for making it through to the end of *Computer Networking Beginners Guide: What is the computer network and how to learn it in a simple way. The Easy step by step Guide for beginners*, let's hope it was informative and able to provide you with all of the tools you need to achieve your goals whatever they may be.

Computer Networking enables us to share resources and use data no matter what scale of architecture you might have. It helps us to exchange information between different people and computers. This has been faster and more reliable than the method of manually handing files or mailing it or retrieving a reel of magnetic tape on the other side of a building.

This technology has also let us to share physical resources; computers within a network can now share a printer or storage drives – ones too expensive to have attached to every machine.

In order for you to be online, your computer or smartphone is connected to a large, distributed network, called the internet. The internet is arranged as an ever-enlarging web of interconnected devices.

The World Wide Web is not the same thing as the internet, even though people often use the two terms interchangeably.

The World Wide Web runs on top of the internet, in the same way as Skype or Instagram do. The internet is the underlying plumbing that conveys all the data for all these applications. These are some of the technologies that keeps us connected online.

Finally, if you found this book useful in any way, a review on Amazon is always appreciated!

www.ingramcontent.com/pod-product-compliance
Lightning Source LLC
LaVergne TN
LVHW051239050326
832903LV00028B/2473

* 9 7 8 1 7 0 3 4 2 6 1 9 9 *